THE MURDER OF
MAGGIE HUME

COLD CASE IN BATTLE CREEK

BLAINE PARDOE and **VICTORIA HESTER**

Charleston · London

THE
History
PRESS

Published by The History Press
Charleston, SC 29403
www.historypress.net

First published 2014

Manufactured in the United States

ISBN 978.1.62619.527.1

Library of Congress CIP data applied for.

To Maggie Hume. We didn't know you, but we will never forget you.

CONTENTS

ACKNOWLEDGEMENTS

When you work on a project like this, you have to start with an open mind and go where the evidence takes you. This book took us on a journey as father and daughter. This product is not the book we set out to write; it is much more…much better.

In the writing of this book, we have consolidated some of the interviews of witnesses to make the flow of the text easier. In this particular case, some witnesses were interviewed three or more times, and detailing those in the book chronologically might be confusing for a reader. In order to assist you, we have a detailed timeline in the back of the book to help you reconcile the events.

We were forced to change the name of one person in the book, which is indicated by an asterisk (*). This individual has been interviewed by police several times but has received threats as a result of his cooperation and asked these authors to protect his identity. There were also several people who passed us information under the auspices of anonymity.

Some phrases in the book are used interchangeably, such as Snug Sack/Snuggle Sack. This was a generic term used to describe a light sleeping bag during the period. Since multiple descriptions were used in the police reports, we have opted to keep them all as they appeared.

Many people played a part in the research and preparation of this book. Special thanks goes out to the following:

Mandi Zimmerman, Calhoun County Sheriff's Department, who was one of the first people to reach out and say to us, "You need to look into this

ACKNOWLEDGEMENTS

case." Mandi made some great behind-the-scenes connections that helped make this book practical.

William Howe, formerly of the Calhoun County Prosecutor's Office. To be blunt, this book would have been a struggle without Bill's insights, perspective, history and objectivity. He was our conscience and someone dedicated to the resolution of this case, even in retirement.

John Hume, Maggie's brother, who was kind enough to tolerate our intrusions.

Mary Smock (Landstra), one of Maggie's closest friends and a wonderful source of stories of her dear friend.

Victoria Houser, Battle Creek city clerk, who tolerated us during a blizzard while we performed our research.

Norma Landstra, close friend of the Hume family.

Nancy Mullett, former assistant prosecuting attorney, Battle Creek.

Joe Newman, former sergeant/detective in charge of the Detective Bureau.

Alan Tolf, former detective assigned to the Hume case. Alan was a wonderful source for the early days of the investigation.

Elwood Priess, former investigator on the Hume case.

Jeff Kabot, former assistant prosecuting attorney, Battle Creek. Jeff, like us, buried himself in the details of this case.

Kevin Danielson*.

Mike Sherzer, former Battle Creek police lieutenant and Battle Creek city councilman.

Kathryn Dunham, Kellogg Community College archivist.

Dennis Mullen, former detective assigned to the Hume case.

Jon Sahli, former prosecutor, Calhoun County.

George Livingston, local historian, Willard Library.

Susie Richter, curator, LaPorte County Historical Society.

Stephanie Hsu, photographer.

Carol L. Miknis.

Randy Reinstein, deputy inspector, Battle Creek Police Department.

Rose Pardoe, mother/grandmother of the authors, who helped us with lodging and sending us some research material.

Steve Jones, for his history of the Ritzee chain.

Cyndi Pardoe, who tolerated countless hours of us talking about this book.

INTRODUCTION

I got hot but never got burned
Well, all I know is she should have learned
Get too close you'll fall right in
You should have known, you can't do that now
—"Looking Out for Number One," Cheap Trick

Unsolved murders gnaw at the minds and consciences of people. An unsolved homicide means that someone got away with the worse crime possible—the taking of another human life. They are the things that keep us up at night. These murderers get to continue to live their lives, while the victims and those close to them are left without closure, without justice. These kinds of cases mean that a killer may yet be walking among us. It could be a neighbor, a co-worker or that man ahead of you at Walmart.

People abhor the unsolved cases because it means that our system of law enforcement has somehow failed. We wonder why justice was not served. We want answers and, in the case of a book, a proper ending. We want balance restored in our lives—the gap filled by the loss of an innocent person to be countered with someone being held to account for the crime. If we cannot have justice, we, at least, demand answers.

This has rarely been more accurate than in the case of Maggie Hume. Her family was well known and beloved in the community. The family was integral to the close-knit Catholic community in Battle Creek, especially at St. Philip Catholic School. Here was a young woman, charming and compassionate, who was horribly assaulted and strangled. Her life was a stark contrast to her death. There was a sense of, "If this could happen to these good churchgoing people, it could happen to anyone." Eyes turn to a succession of prosecutors and investigators wondering, "Why didn't anyone ever get brought to trial for this crime?" When answers didn't come, speculation and recrimination filled the emotional gap.

To just lay the blame at the feet of the police and prosecutors isn't fair either. The courts, local and national politicians, defense attorneys and the misguided press all played a role in this denial of justice. As one investigator told us, some of the victim's friends and associates became uncooperative over time. Having moved on from sowing the wild oats of their youth, they had children of their own and didn't want to reopen their own semi-raucous pasts. Certainly we were surprised when some of the individuals we reached out to declined interviews.

What the public knew about the case came from the newspapers and television and was a distorted impression at best. It wasn't the media's fault; few of them ever got exposed to the intricacies of the case. To them, it was merely a story that played out over the decades. There was a confession in the case, but prosecutors did not accept it at face value. The reasons for this were never explained to the public. There were the bizarre links to other murders and crimes in the area. All of this led to more questions than answers.

When we started working on this book, our thinking was that it was an unsolved murder and that the police probably had a pretty good idea of who did it but had never gone public with the information. We were cautioned by investigators that there was more to the story, but they were often vague in their warnings. Once we got into the case, we finally understood. This was a tragic murder that was tied (directly or indirectly, depending on your perspective) to four other deaths. It was a senseless killing that caused a bitter schism between the Calhoun County Prosecutor's Office and the Battle Creek Police Department. It was a tension and conflict that played out to a national audience on television.

What has been lost by some in all of this emotional and political turmoil is the victim of this heinous crime: Maggie Hume.

MAGGIE WAS AN OUTGOING, stubbornly independent girl. She was always up for a good time. She was flirty and fun. She loved her job at Dr. Chadwick's office and enjoyed living in her own apartment with her roommate, Margaret. She was described by many as a "good person" and "fun loving." She was so young and so full of life. And that life was taken from her.

Maggie Hume in 1980. *Courtesy of Mary Smock (Landstra).*

Maggie enjoyed taking dancing classes with a close family friend, Mary Smock (Landstra), for years. The Landstra family met the Hume family at a local dance club. Once the mothers became friends, their families soon followed. It was usual for both families to pack up and spend summer days at the Riverside Swim Club. The families became so close that the Landstras bought a house that ran up to the Hume household and often spent holidays together. "Hardly a month doesn't go by when I don't think about her," Mary Smock said of Maggie. She had that kind of impact on those around her.

In reading police reports and interviewing people, no fewer than three individuals claimed that Maggie was their best friend. This is a testimony to her outgoing character and personality.

Mary described her favorite memory of Maggie:

> *When we went to Florida together, she was sixteen or so and I was one year younger than her. We went down because her grandma and grandpa had a condo down there. We hung out and had fun for a week. We got caught mixing drinks by her grandma, who told us, "You girls take those glasses and head off for bed." They were nervous about us. We went out and sat on a wall outside of the condo, watching the guys drive by in Firebirds, waving to us and flirting with us. Her grandma actually went out in her car, laid down in the car seat out of sight, just to be near us to make sure nothing happened. We had a blast.*

Maggie Hume in happier times. *Courtesy of Mary Smock (Landstra).*

Introduction

During her four years of high school at St. Philip Catholic High School, Maggie was described as a good student. She was in the honor society but didn't run with the popular crowd. She had started at the private school in seventh grade, and most of the cliques had already formed in the small school. She also was the daughter of the school's football coach; some of the other students felt that she got preferential treatment since her dad was the coach. She was a cheerleader all of her high school years, but some hinted that she got that because of her father's role.

Family and church meant a great deal to Maggie. The weekend before her demise, she double-dated with her brother, John. They went to Cedar Point for a fun-filled day riding roller coasters.

Maggie Hume graduated high school and continued her education at Kellogg Community College (KCC), where she later met Jay Carter. She was independent, moving out of her parents house, and was just starting her own life. Maggie eked out a living paycheck to paycheck and enjoyed every moment of it. A fun-loving good Catholic girl was ripped from her family, friends and community. At only twenty years old, she was just starting the rest of her life.

That summer of 1982, her last one, was one that would be frozen in time for her, her friends and family.

MAGGIE'S MISSING

Sleep like a child resting deep
You don't know what you give me I keep
For these moments alone.
—*"Sweet Dreams," Air Supply*

Summers in Michigan are fickle things, and the summer of 1982 was no exception. Thanks to the influence of Lake Michigan, the weather in western Michigan is hard (if not impossible) to predict. You can suffer through two weeks of drought followed by a week of torrential rain and ground-shaking thunderstorms. The week of August 17, 1982, in Battle Creek, Michigan, was no different. The week before, it had been rainy, but for three days, the temperatures had been hot and dry and in the middle eighties, with the nights dropping to seventy degrees. People were in a constant state of opening and closing windows and turning air conditioners on and off.

For relaxation and a chance to cool off during the days, people flocked to Willard Beach at Goguac Lake. Nights allowed you to go to the Battle Creek Drive-in Theater or the West Point—if you were willing to tolerate the mosquitoes. The movies were always a chance to sit in some cool air, and the second week of August 1982 had a mixed bag of films. *An Officer and a Gentleman* had just opened the weekend before at the West Columbia Theaters—the perfect date movie. The musical comedy *The Best Little Whorehouse in Texas*, with Burt Reynolds and Dolly Parton, played there, too. If these didn't appeal to your tastes, *E.T. the Extraterrestrial* was still playing for its eleventh consecutive week. In the 1980s, films didn't appear in theaters for three weeks and then two months later on iTunes, Redbox or BluRay. They ran for weeks at a time, and it was typical for people to go see the same movie several times over.

Some teens took the time to paint "the Rock," a boulder outside town along the I-194 into the city (known humorously as "the Penetrator" because it was the one way into the city that avoided the spider web of train tracks that contorted around the city). The boulder alternated almost every weekend with something new sloppily painted on it. Done at night, usually with alcohol involved, the Rock was both a rite of passage and public statement at the same time.

Television was in the peak of reruns. Glossy dramas dealing with wealth or corny situation comedies with laugh tracks dominated people's TV viewing. *Dallas*, *Three's Company*, *The Jeffersons*, *Joanie Loves Chachi* and *The Dukes of Hazard* topped the television lineup. They were a mindless form of escapism from the heat and humidity of the late Michigan summer.

The only other form of entertainment that week of August was the Calhoun County Fair in Marshall. As Michigan's oldest county fair, it was a natural draw if you were young and attempting to enjoy those last few days of summer. The county fair marked a turning point—the last benchmark day on the calendar before school started up. For Battle Creek residents, it provided a much-needed diversion to a long summer.

Whatever the trends were in the nation, it always seemed that Battle Creek was a year or two behind. While disco was dying elsewhere, a few dance clubs were just opening in Cereal City. Battle Creek always had a feeling of being out of sync with the rest of the world.

From a historical perspective, August 1982 was a quiet month. Coke had released a new product, Diet Coke, that month, offering people an alternative to Tab Cola. The month saw the release of a new technology, compact disks, dooming the vinyl records albums to obscurity. On the other side of the globe, the month of August found Iran and Iraq embroiled in a bloody war. August 1982 wasn't one of those months where history changed dramatically or key world events altered our perceptions. It was the end of another typical, almost mundane Michigan summer—quiet… unobtrusive…benign.

It was not so quiet in Battle Creek, however, on Wednesday, August 18, 1982. The relatively peaceful summer month was shaken when Margaret "Maggie" Mary Hume didn't show up to work in the morning.

COLD CASE IN BATTLE CREEK

MAGGIE HUME DIDN'T MISS work unless she was sick. By all accounts, Maggie loved her job. She had graduated Kellogg Community College's program for medical secretaries and relished her job as a receptionist at Dr. John Chadwick's office. She was supposed to have been at the office at 9:00 a.m. but didn't come in or call. Dr. Chadwick had even placed a call to Maggie's father, Mike Hume, who said that he didn't know where his daughter was. There was not a mad rush to find out where she was; her roommate, Margaret Van Winkle, was scheduled to come in as a patient that morning anyway. Perhaps she knew where Maggie was.

When Margaret arrived, Angie Henderson, who worked at Dr. Chadwick's as well, asked her if Maggie was ill. "No," Margaret replied. Angie and Maggie alternated coming into work at Dr. Chadwick's office, and on this Wednesday, Angie was the one to come in early and Maggie was due to arrive at 9:00 a.m. but had not come in yet.

As a matter of fact, Margaret hadn't seen Maggie at all in the apartment they shared at 55 Stringham Road that morning. Margaret had gotten in only a few hours earlier; she had been on a trip to pick up her sister, Emily, at Detroit Metro Airport (she was coming back from a trip to Europe, and her flight had been delayed). Margaret had arrived at their apartment at 4:00 a.m. and had gone straight to bed. When she woke up, Maggie was nowhere to be seen. Margaret suggested that the receptionist call Virgil "Jay" Carter, Maggie's boyfriend. Perhaps she had spent the night with him, or if not, he may know where Maggie was.

Number 55 Stringham Road was part of a complex of apartments known as the River Apartments. Poised several hundred feet from the Kalamazoo River, the apartments at the time were inexpensively built in Battle Creek's Urbandale neighborhood. They had thin walls and were geared for people on fixed incomes or young adults who were looking to live on their own. Only a few minutes from downtown Battle Creek, they were perfect as a first apartment—just enough living until you could save up some money and move someplace nicer.

Angie Henderson called Jay Carter and informed him that Maggie was not at work and inquired as to where she was. Jay said that he didn't know where she was but also didn't seem to be worried at the time. Between 10:30 a.m. and 11:00 a.m., when Maggie still had not appeared, Margaret called Jay herself to tell him that Maggie still had not been located. Margaret relayed to Jay that she had not seen Maggie when she had arrived at the apartment at about 4:00 a.m.

Number 55 Stringham Road in Battle Creek the afternoon Maggie's body was discovered. *Provided via FOIA, Battle Creek Police Department.*

Jay would later inform police that he went to St. Philip High School in search of Maggie's father. He said that he entered the school and spoke to people there looking for Mr. Hume, but no one knew where he was at the time.

What we do know is that near 11:15 a.m., Jay arrived at the Hume house on Central Street. He found John Hume, Maggie's younger seventeen-year-old brother, and told him that Maggie was apparently missing. The last time John had seen his sister was when they had double-dated the Saturday before at Cedar Point amusement park. Jay and John traveled to St. Philip High School, Battle Creek's lone Catholic high school, where Jay claimed he had been earlier. Maggie's father, Mike Hume, was the athletic director and football coach at St. Phil, and while school was not yet in session, he was preparing for another season of Tiger Football.

On the way to St. Phil, Jay told John that he had already been to the high school looking for his father but had not been able to locate him. When they did find Mike Hume in his office, Jay didn't seem surprised at all. Mike had a set of keys to Maggie's apartment. He told John and Jay to go over to the apartment and look around. For the time being, Mike remained at St. Phil.

With the spare keys in hand, John and Jay went to 55 Stringham Road, apartment no. 19. On the way, Jay had told John that he wanted "to look

Outside of apartment no. 19, the scene of the crime. *Provided via FOIA, Battle Creek Police Department.*

for clues." Maggie's dark green AMC Hornet was parked outside, and they checked the vehicle but found no sign of her. John unlocked the front door and went in. The apartment was not cleaned or straightened, but that was not out of the ordinary. This was, after all, the apartment of two young women out on their own for the first time. There was an uncashed check sitting on the dining table, undisturbed. The two men turned on the lights and went straight to Maggie's bedroom. Her alarm clock was going off. One of them shut off the beeping.

John noticed his sister's glasses on the nightstand. The glasses had big lenses, and their presence there caught John's attention. Maggie was nearly blind without her glasses. "She could not find her way around the room without her glasses," John would later tell officers.

John's eyes turned toward her bed. It was disheveled. The fitted sheet had been sprung on all four corners. John made a comment to Jay about how messy the bed was, but Jay assured him that he had seen it that messy before. John disagreed with his assessment. Maggie could be messy, that much he

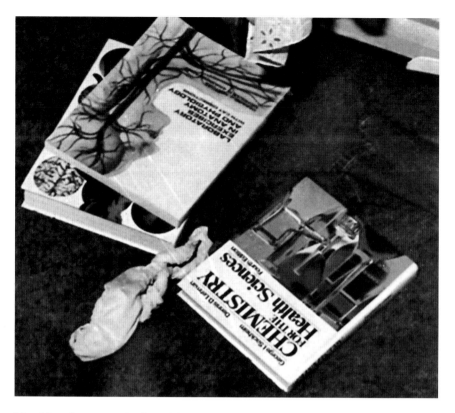

Maggie's underpants on the floor of her room. *Provided via FOIA, Battle Creek Police Department.*

knew, but not like this. The doors to Maggie's closet were opened. John noticed a Snug Sack sleeping bag on the floor, but at his glance, it looked like simply part of the floor of closet rather than something placed there.

John stayed in Maggie's bathroom to look for anything that might be an indication as to where his sister was. Jay went to Margaret's bedroom for a few moments. Jay then returned to Maggie's bedroom, while John looked in Margaret's bedroom. When John returned, he found Jay on his knees at the closet entrance. He was pulling a pale-green nightgown from the pile of blankets and clothing on the floor of the closet. Jay told John he couldn't remember what nightgown she had been wearing the night before. Jay pulled out the blue and white checkered one from the clothes on the floor of the closet but said that he was not sure which one she had changed into. Jay told John that he had been looking in the closet for her shoes, to see what pair she might have on.

Both young men noticed that Maggie's purse was nowhere to be seen. Perhaps she had taken it with her, wherever she had gone? The two of them

Margaret Van Winkle's bedroom as it appeared the day after the murder. Margaret slept for a few hours that morning, not realizing that her roommate was dead only a few feet away. Her nervousness prodded officers into finding the body. *Provided via FOIA, Battle Creek Police Department.*

left her bedroom and went to check the patio. The apartment had a small balcony with a screened window and a door leading into the living room. The two went onto the patio to see if there was any sign of the screen having been tampered with. The screen was quite intact, but there were some screws on the patio. John remembered that Margaret had told them they had been working on their grill a few days earlier and that the screws most likely had come from that grill repair.

There was no sign of Maggie in the apartment, but with her glasses and car there, it was clear that she had not just taken off to run a quick errand.

Jay and John drove back to St. Philip and returned to Mike Hume, who was at the school in his office between running football practices. They told him about their search and that his daughter was still missing. Mike said that they needed to go to the police station and file a missing person report.

They arrived at the Battle Creek Police Department and spoke with officers there. Jay offered that the last time he had seen Maggie had been at 11:30 p.m. the night before. Since that time, the trio did not know of anyone who had seen her.

The officers gathered the basic information on Maggie—age twenty years; five feet, six inches tall; and about 135 to 140 pounds in weight. She had brown, almost reddish hair and hazel eyes. The only identifying mark on her was a small scar on the calf of one of her legs. Mike gave officers a photo from his wallet of his daughter to assist in their search. One of the men who engaged with Mike early on was Elwood Priess. The officer had been with the Battle Creek Police Department since 1967, having moved down from Newberry in Michigan's Upper Peninsula. He had served as an MP (Military Police) in the army before joining the Battle Creek Police Department. Priess had known Mike Hume personally for some time. He was an avid follower of St. Philip's football program. When he wasn't attending games, he was working with the school as security and had gotten to know the coach quite well. "The chief pulled me in when they came into the department because I knew them. He thought I could be a liaison with the family."

The officers spoke with Mike about Maggie's home life. Was there any friction between the family and Maggie? No. Mike only expressed deep concern over the welfare of his daughter. The investigator's focus shifted to Maggie's boyfriend, Jay Carter. The athletic twenty-one-year-old Kellogg Community College (KCC) student was asked if they had any problems with their relationship, such as a fight or anything to that effect. Jay said no, there had not been any major disagreements.

The young man also offered a tantalizing clue. Jay said that while he had been with Maggie the night before, she had received a phone call at about 10:30 p.m. He said that it had sounded like a black male on the phone asking for "my baby Maggie." She had related to him that it was not an obscene call but rather was more of a nuisance.

The officers placed a call to Maggie's roommate, Margaret, at work. Usually, Margaret was at home in the evenings, but the night before had been a very rare exception. She had placed a phone call to Maggie to tell her that her sister's flight had been delayed at Detroit Metro Airport and that she wouldn't be back until around 4:30 a.m.

They asked Margaret if anything had seemed out of place in the apartment that morning. She did note that the closet doors in the hallway, directly across from Maggie's room, had been left open. She had noticed that Maggie's room had been disheveled more than usual. Margaret had said that she was not entirely surprised that her roommate was not in bed when she had been there in the morning. Maggie stayed with Jay occasionally.

Even for the officers taking notes, things were not adding up. The dispatcher put out an announcement regarding Maggie so that the entire police force was aware that she was missing. They asked Margaret if they could meet her at the apartment and conduct a search for themselves. She agreed to meet with them during her lunch break, at about 12:45 p.m. Priess suggested to Mike that he go home and stand by the phone in case Maggie called. There was little that could be done sitting at the station. John and Jay also went to the Hume residence. Jay brought up the phone call that Maggie had received the night before. Now, away from the police, the call seemed more sinister. Jay said that the caller said "some crude things he wanted to do to Maggie."

Once back at the Hume house, the phone rang. It was from Maggie's former boyfriend, Jim Downey. Jim and Maggie had dated when they were in high school and had remained good friends. Maggie had placed a beer order with him for her roommate's upcoming birthday party, and Jim wanted to firm up the delivery. Jim's brother, Norm, owned the Lakeview Lounge, and Jim had secured a keg of beer for the party. John quickly relayed that no one knew where Maggie was.

Margaret arrived to meet Patrolman Bill Brenner and Detective Pestun at her apartment at 12:50 p.m. accompanied by a co-worker. She unlocked the door and allowed the officers to enter. They noticed several used bowls and dishes left on coffee tables and unwashed pots and pans in the kitchen. They asked Margaret if that was uncommon, and she said that was not unusual. She did reiterate that the closet door being left open *was* something out of the ordinary.

Moving into Maggie's room, she noticed her roomie's eyeglasses on the small night table and said that this was not like Maggie. They asked if Maggie had an emergency pair of glasses or if she wore contacts. Maggie did have a spare pair of glasses in the medicine cabinet in the bathroom. Patrolman Brenner went in and found them. Maggie didn't wear contacts. Margaret said that even if Maggie got up in the middle of the night to use the bathroom, she had to wear her glasses to see.

Margaret noticed that while Maggie's purse was missing, her keys were still on her dresser. They asked Margaret to check the closets to make sure that nothing was missing. Patrolman Brenner went along with her. She gave a cursory look in Maggie's closet and her own. The only thing she noticed not hanging in Maggie's closet was a blue nightgown that she often wore. The Snuggle Sack comforter and blanket on the floor of Maggie's closet didn't seem to attract her attention.

When they returned to the kitchen, Detective Pestun was on the telephone with Sergeant Burdett, filling him in on their findings thus far. Margaret

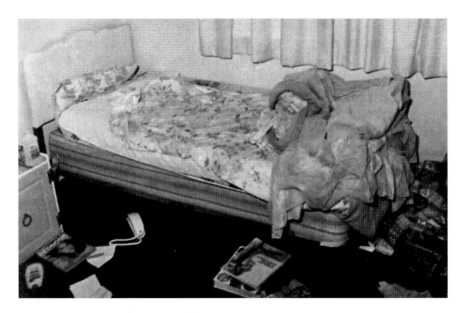

Maggie's bedroom as the police found it the afternoon after her murder. *Provided via FOIA, Battle Creek Police Department.*

asked the officer if he would look around the apartment one more time to make sure there wasn't anything there that shouldn't be. Margaret's nervousness or perhaps her intuition kicked in. Her comment was along the lines of, "I don't want to open a closet door or find a body under a bed or behind a couch." It was clear that she didn't feel that they had done an adequate job of performing a search.

So, to appease the jittery nerves of the young woman, Brenner looked behind the couch. He then went into Margaret's room and looked in her closet and then under her bed. He went into Maggie's room and noticed again how messy the bed appeared. Her pillow had been stuffed between the mattress and the headboard. He glanced into the closet and saw that the floor was covered with what appeared to be dirty clothing and a comforter. The clothing and comforter drew his attention.

Returning to the kitchen, he spoke to Margaret about the comforter. The red, white and blue quilt-like comforter was something that Maggie usually kept folded on the beanbag chair at the foot of her bed, according to her roommate. "It's strange that her quilt is lying on that long pile of clothes in the closet." Officer Brenner reassured her that he would recheck the closet. Bending down, he moved the quilt and observed that under it was a pink and

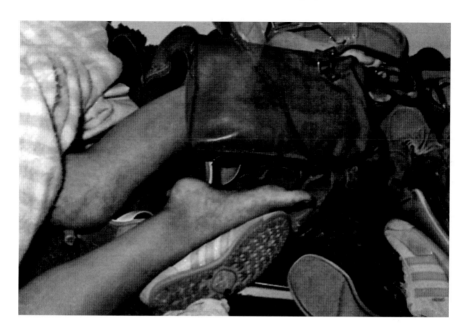

Maggie Hume in the closet. Jay Carter was looking for her shoes in the closet. He would have noticed her legs while looking for the shoes, but mysteriously, he didn't. He also did not see Maggie's purse. *Provided via FOIA, Battle Creek Police Department.*

white blanket. Slowly reaching down, he touched and felt something hard. Carefully, he pulled up the edge of the blanket and observed a bare human leg. Margaret's worst fears had been confirmed.

The situation had just changed. This was no longer a missing person issue; the dead body concealed in the closet pointed to something entirely different: murder. Brenner went back to join Detective Pestun and whispered to him that he believed he had found Maggie Hume. He spoke in such a manner as to avoid alarming her roommate. Pestum asked him if he was sure. He nodded that he was.

Margaret could sense that something was wrong, either from the facial expressions of the officers or their low-talking tone. She called out to them, "Somebody please talk to me!" Brenner told Margaret and her companion that it appeared they had found Maggie Hume.

Number 55 Stringham Road, apartment no. 19, had just become the only active murder scene investigation in the city of Battle Creek.

THE START OF THE INVESTIGATION

After all that we've been through, I will make it up to you. I promise to.
And after all that's been said and done,
You're just the part of me I can't let go.
— "Hard to Say I'm Sorry," Chicago

The history of Battle Creek's law enforcement can be traced back to 1850. Battle Creek was formed as a community in 1833. It began as the township of Milton, but by 1836, it had grown to nearly five hundred and was renamed as Battle Creek. The village of Battle Creek was created in 1850, and with that formation, the village treasurer was required to also fill the role of village marshal. The first such marshal was Franklin S. Clarke. The role was not as much law enforcement as it was keeper of the peace. Seven men held the title between 1850 and 1858.

After that brief period, the population had grown enough for Battle Creek to reorganize as a city. This, in turn, led to the formal role of city marshal, the first one being Moses B. Russell. In 1900, the city council authorized the creation of the first true Battle Creek Police Department. The first chief was the last of the long line of marshals, William Farrington. Chief Farrington was authorized to hire nine policemen, and they established their headquarters at 25–27 Main Street, known today as Michigan Avenue. The department grew with the city. In 1911, it purchased its first patrol car, which doubled as an ambulance. In 1930, a formal Detective Bureau was established. By 1982, the department had become well established.

THE MURDER OF MAGGIE HUME

The chief at the time of the Hume murder was Thomas Thear. Before relocating to Battle Creek, he had been a deputy commander in Montgomery, Maryland, and a deputy chief in Burlington, Vermont. He was an outsider to Battle Creek and the men he commanded.

Like most chiefs, he reorganized the department to fit the ever-evolving thinking around law enforcement. As Detective Al Tolf conveyed, "Detectives used to have certain cases as specialties—some homicide, some B&E [breaking and entering], some checks. He restructured us around districts. Each detective had a district and was responsible for the crimes in their district. Nick Pestun had the district in Urbandale and was the lead on this case." Detective Pestun had a great deal of experience in the department, but not with homicides. His true strength was property crimes. From most accounts from officers who were attached to the case, this was either his first or second murder case where he had the lead, and as such, it would suffer from his lack of experience in those first critical hours and days.

The investigation into the death of Maggie Hume got off to a bad start almost immediately. When Patrolman Bill Brenner left after finding the body in the bedroom, he closed the door behind him. Detective Pestun wanted to go back into the room and check the body for himself but

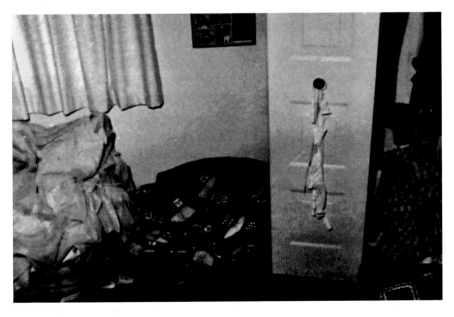

Maggie's bedroom as the police found it. Note the Snuggle Sack and blanket in the closet that conceal her body. *Provided via FOIA, Battle Creek Police Department.*

couldn't, as Brenner had accidentally locked the door. For the first few minutes after finding Maggie's body, the police couldn't even get to it. The building manager had to be found so that he could unlock the door at about 1:20 p.m.

Detectives Baker and Priess arrived shortly thereafter and were informed that Maggie's body had been found. Other officers arrived as well when Detectives Tolf, Donald Yesh and Michael VanStratton also came to the apartment. The medical examiner, Dr. Cassin, then arrived. It was standard procedure to have the medical examiner come to help preserve evidence and to officially declare the victim dead. The process took time as the detectives worked carefully to preserve evidence.

Her body was almost tucked into a quilted sleeping bag—a "Snuggie" (or Snuggle) Sack. The detectives then began to remove the clothing on top of her as well as on the floor, as if they were carefully dismantling a jigsaw puzzle. A green hooded robe was extracted from the closet next, followed by a white dress with purple, yellow and pink stripes. A white terry cloth jacket was pulled out along with a smock and a lavender sweater. A light-green nightgown was gently removed, and a blue checked nightgown was pulled out. Much of the clothing was wedged in and on top of the body. Another nightgown with the word "Snooz" was on it, and there was a white bra. A pair of gray slacks and a belt, along with a white print top, were near her torso. There were no empty hangers, so the clothing was presumed to have been dirty clothes, awaiting a laundry day that would never come.

As they worked their way down, the detectives found the purse, which Jay had indicated was missing, under Maggie's body. The wallet and checkbook were missing out of it.

A pink checkered blanket had been draped over her torso and legs. Maggie wore an aqua and white checkered nightgown with no undergarments. Detective Yesh oversaw the careful gathering of the material in the closet so that it could be tested for trace evidence later. The detectives had her hands taped in plastic bags in case there were hairs or scrapings under her fingernails from her assailant. She lay on the floor of the closet on top of a plastic laundry container with her legs on top of her shoes. Maggie's head was turned to the right, facing outward from the closet. There were indications on her neck of lines indicating potential strangulation.

Livor mortis, the settling of blood upon death, had indicated that her death had come hours earlier. The things that she lay on top of were imprinted as white on her flesh against the contrast of the purple tint of her skin. The marks around her neck stood out as reddish. With her red hair tossed aside, it was hard to imagine her as the image that people recognized. There were signs of sexual assault as well, proof that the last minutes of her life had been a deadly struggle.

At 3:46 p.m., two EMS technicians, Scott Brockman and Allen Egnatuk, arrived to remove her body to take her on the ten-minute ride to Leila Hospital for a postmortem examination and final identification.

Her bedroom had a single window, with the curtains drawn, that faced out onto the patio. Next to her bed was a bright-yellow nightstand. Her single twin bed was located along the west wall of the apartment, with the headboard facing to the south. The fitted sheets were pulled up in the corners of her bed, indicating a struggle. Along the east wall of the bedroom was a chest of drawers and a shelf-case. On the floor was a telephone, the latest issue of *Redbook* magazine and several college textbooks from Maggie's courses at KCC. Also on the floor was a pink top, a pair of jeans and a rolled-up pair of underpants. A bra hung from the small knob on the closet door. The door itself was one of those that folded when it slid open.

Hanging on the wall was a collage of photographs from Maggie's life. The images were of much happier times with her family and friends—staring silently into the room where she had been found.

Next to Maggie's nightstand is the phone, which was discovered off the hook. *Provided via FOIA, Battle Creek Police Department.*

Maggie's pink top and jeans, casually tossed on the floor of her bedroom. *Provided via FOIA, Battle Creek Police Department.*

Nick Pestun went onto the balcony to inspect it as a possible entry site. Looking down, he noticed that there were footprints on the utility boxes, as if someone had used them as steps in climbing onto the balcony. Several latent fingerprints were discovered as well, one of which was found on the balcony door on the inside of the apartment.

The apartment was, for a brief few hours, frozen in time. It had been left as it had appeared when Margaret had led officers through it a few hours earlier. Dirty pots and pans were left in the kitchen. Bowls used for popcorn and soup were left on the coffee tables in the living area. Maggie's car keys were on her dresser in plain sight, along with an uncashed check on the dining table. Also, all of the keys were accounted for, which meant that whoever left the apartment had done so via the balcony—otherwise they would not have been able to deadbolt-lock the door to the apartment, which was how Margaret had found it locked.

The pillow in Maggie's room was wedged between the headboard and the mattress. According to Margaret, this was done to muffle the sounds when Jay and Maggie had sex in the room. Three chairs sat around the tiny secondhand dining table in the kitchenette. Newspapers were located where they had fallen from the coffee table onto the dull, dirty red carpeting.

At the Hume house, the phone had been ringing as family members learned of what had happened. One call that came in was from Maggie's former

The kitchen area of Maggie's apartment. *Provided via FOIA, Battle Creek Police Department.*

The living room in apartment no. 19, showing the popcorn and soup bowls that remained from the night before. *Provided via FOIA, Battle Creek Police Department.*

A detailed view of the closet, apparently after the removal of the victim. *Provided via FOIA, Battle Creek Police Department.*

boyfriend, Jim Downey following up on his earlier call regarding beer. Jim numbly hung up upon hearing the news that his former girlfriend was dead.

The other detectives, led by VanStratton, began to take careful photographs of the tiny apartment. VanStratton noticed that there were fresh grass clippings in Maggie's bedroom, including some on her blue jeans on the floor. He followed the trail from the bedroom, back down the hall past Margaret Van Winkle's bedroom, into the living area and right up to the door leading to the balcony. Combined with the footprints that Pestun had located, it was clear that someone had climbed up on the balcony and entered the apartment through the door there. Whoever it was had not gone into Margaret's bedroom but had instead gone straight to Maggie's bedroom. Samples of the grass clippings were gathered for study as well.

One detective, Elwood Priess, who had agreed to be the liaison with the Hume family, assumed the painful duty of going to the Hume home on Central Street and telling them that Maggie had been found. "I was there after Bill Brenner found the body. When I got there, I was followed pretty quickly by the medical examiner. Well, I went to the Hume house to tell Mike. It was one of the hardest things I have ever had to do—next to dealing with my brother's death. You could tell in his face that he knew what happened…that we had found her."

Lorie Hume, Maggie's mother, found out when she returned from a trip to Comstock at about 2:30 p.m. in the afternoon. Mike came out while she was in the car and told her, "We have to be strong, Maggie was murdered last night." Mrs. Hume thought it was a horrible joke at first. She didn't remember going into the house. She sat for hours on the couch as a steady stream of support poured in from the tight-knit St. Philip community.

At 4:00 p.m., the intercom to the apartment buzzed. The man began to walk away, but officers followed him. It was Raymond Kosak. Confused by the sudden police attention, he explained that he was an old friend of Maggie's who lived in Florida. When he was in town, he would stop in and visit her. He had last spoken with her on the previous Friday night on the telephone. The officers let Kosak go, promising to follow up with him later.

While there was a large police presence at the River Apartments, the officers did not begin to canvass the other apartments until just after 4:00 p.m., when Pestun, Baker and Priess led the effort. Maggie's neighbors would each learn of her death and offer whatever tidbits they could. Detective Al Tolf headed back to the station to interview Jay Carter and Margaret Van Winkle at 4:32 p.m.

One of the first things officers do is to attempt to reconstruct the last day or so of the victim's life. Who did she interact with? Where was she at what time? Also, it was critical in such cases to talk to the people closest to the victim quickly, to get their story. Oftentimes, one of these people may have actually been the perpetrator of the crime, so getting their story early allows the investigation to validate their facts.

Detective Tolf was interested in getting to the basics. Virgil Jay Carter was not a Battle Creek resident. He was from Westville, Indiana, and had been dating Maggie for two years. They had met up at Kellogg Community College where Jay was one of the top players on the college's volleyball team. He was older than Maggie by just over a year. Jay said that he and Maggie were planning on getting married in a year or two.

Jay said that it was normal for the two of them to visit every night. The hours of his visits varied depending on when he got off work at the Beer Company. The night before, Jay said that he had gotten off of work at about 10:00 p.m. and drove directly over to Maggie's apartment. Her car wasn't there, so he drove over to the Ritzee in Urbandale, just up the road from the apartment, to call her.

The Ritzee chain of restaurants was an icon in Mid and Western Michigan. Jim Messenger had been the original owner of the chain, starting in fifty post exchanges during World War II—including one in nearby Fort Custer. Steve

Jones started work for him and turned the chain into a more standardized restaurant. It was like a half dozen other chains that sprung up around the same time as McDonald's. In Battle Creek, the Ritzee was known for its crinkle-cut French fries. Under Jones's leadership, the restaurant opened the first drive-thru ordering system in the city. Half-price days at the Ritzee had cars lined up for more than a half a mile to go in. The Ritzee was known as a place for kids to go for an inexpensive meal or just to hang out—it had been that way for generations in Battle Creek.

According to Jay, while there that night, Maggie drove by and spotted him. Jay questioned her as to where she had been, and she had said that she had been with her friend and co-worker Leigh Wilson. Maggie also mentioned that she smelled smoke in her car, and Jay agreed to check it. He couldn't see any issues, but the parking lot of the Ritzee was not well lit. He suggested that they check it out at her apartment. Both of them drove their respective cars over to her apartment, where Jay popped the hood but could not find the source of the odor that Maggie had smelled.

They went upstairs to the apartment, and along the way, Maggie asked him if he would spend the night. Jay thought that was strange; usually it was *him* asking *her* to spend the night. They went inside the apartment and had

Maggie's AMC Hornet. Jay Carter claimed that she felt it was producing a smell of oil, but no evidence of this was ever found. *Provided via FOIA, Battle Creek Police Department.*

intercourse in the living room, again a departure for the two of them—he assumed it was because her roomie, Margaret, was out of town. While Maggie went to the restroom, Jay made himself some dinner, a can of soup.

Margaret called while Jay was there, telling Maggie that her sister's flight from Europe was delayed and that she would not be home until 3:00 or 4:00 a.m.; she told Maggie not to be concerned if she heard any noises at that hour—it was just her coming in late.

The living room area of Maggie's apartment. *Provided via FOIA, Battle Creek Police Department.*

Another telephone call came in—one that Maggie took. According to Jay, the caller was a black man asking for "my sweet Maggie." Maggie simply hung up the phone, giving Jay "a funny look." Jay said that he didn't listen to the call; he only got the information from Maggie after she had hung up.

They sat on the couch together, with Jay eventually making some popcorn for them. Each of them had a bowl and sat at opposing ends of the couch. They watched *M*A*S*H* and the news. Jay indicated that he left the apartment sometime after the news. When he last saw her, she was wearing a light-green or light-blue nylon waist-length nightgown. Before he left, he said that Maggie had complained of being cold. He had gone to the hallway closet and had taken out a pink and white checkered blanket with which to cover her. Jay didn't remember if he had closed the hallway closet door or not. Maggie walked him to the door, and he heard her lock it behind him. Jay said that Maggie was always very careful about locking the doors to her apartment.

Jay retold the story to Detective Tolf of how he had been called from Dr. Chadwick's office. He had told her work that she may have had car trouble and that she had not been feeling well the night before, so perhaps she was sick. After he got the next call from the doctor's office, at about 10:30 or 11:00 a.m., he went over to the apartment with John Hume (after going to St. Philip to get the keys from Maggie's father) and checked the apartment. Jay reaffirmed that her bed was in disarray. They had found Maggie's glasses, which had been a concern given her weak eyesight.

He had seen a pair of rolled-up underpants on the floor that he said were the same ones she had been wearing the night before. He admitted that he had looked into the closet and saw her nightgown in a pile of clothes in the closet. Jay also said that he knew that her purse was missing. He and John had checked the balcony, but everything appeared in order, although he could not remember if it was locked. Jay also mentioned that a tan flight bag seemed to be missing—perhaps stolen.

Jay informed Detective Tolf that he had handled some papers that were lying on the floor of Maggie's room, thinking that she might have written a note as to her whereabouts. When asked about the checkbook, he said that she did have one that she always carried in her purse. She also had a twenty-point diamond ring that she carried in a bank envelop in her purse. Maggie always wore a thin gold pre-engagement ring with a small diamond on her left hand.

When Detective Tolf asked who Jay thought might have a reason to want to harm her, he offered up several names: Phil Mitchell, Jim Downey and Tom Carpenter. After their short interview, the first of several, Jay was dismissed.

The discussion with Margaret Van Winkle was focused more on the condition and state of the apartment when she came home that night. The lights were not on when she came in, and the door was double-locked. The drapes were drawn. The hallway light offered her a glimpse into Maggie's room. Maggie normally left her bedroom door open. Margaret saw that the bed was unmade, which was also not out of the ordinary. She didn't remember if Maggie's closet door was open or not. When prompted about the tan flight bag, she did say that Maggie used the bag to transport albums and that, apparently, the bag and about fifteen albums were missing.

There were times when Maggie did carry large sums of cash home to make a deposit in the morning for Dr. Chadwick. A check was made with Dr. Chadwick, however, and Maggie had not been carrying any money for a deposit. It was hard to believe that someone would kill her for the paltry amount of money in her purse at the time.

The last time Margaret had seen Maggie was when she left for the airport at 6:30 p.m. At that time, Maggie had been wearing a pink polo shirt, jeans and no shoes and had been on her bed reading a magazine. Margaret had called Maggie from the airport at about 10:15 p.m. to let her know that she would be late. Maggie didn't indicate whether Jay was in the apartment. She did tell Maggie to not be concerned if she heard noises in the early morning hours, or something to that effect.

Detective Tolf asked Margaret questions regarding Maggie's relationship with Jay Carter. According to her, Jay and Maggie had been dating since November 1980. Maggie had been working at KCC and had met Jay there. Jay came over almost every night between 8:00 and 8:30 p.m. Jay had given Maggie a pre-engagement ring in April 1982.

The relationship between the two of them had been anything but smooth. Margaret's description of their relationship was "hot and cold." Despite this, she assumed that the two of them would eventually get married. There had been a big argument in June 1982 about the two of them getting married in a Catholic church, something that Maggie was adamant about. Maggie told her that she wouldn't marry Jay if there wasn't a Catholic wedding. Maggie's will was clear in what she told her roommate: "He'd have to get used to that situation." Jay had sent her flowers one or two times after they had fought. This was not their only argument. According to Margaret, Maggie and Jay were constantly arguing. When asked about Maggie's personality, she replied, "Maggie is very *very* set in her ways."

The question was asked: "Did she say that she might not marry Jay?" "Yes…if he didn't change his ideas and get married in the Catholic Church."

Maggie and Jim Downey, her former boyfriend. *Courtesy of Willard Library, Helen Warner Branch.*

Margaret had set her alarm clock for 6:45 a.m. and had slept through the alarm, having only gone to bed a few hours earlier. She woke up at 7:57 a.m. in a panic and ran into Maggie's bedroom because it had the closest telephone. The phone was off the hook and beeping on the floor. Margaret called her supervisor, Marge Warren, and told her that she would be late. In a flurry of speed, she got dressed and left the apartment at 8:25 a.m. At that time, she didn't notice whether Maggie's alarm was beeping.

The detective probed carefully. Was Maggie seeing anyone other than Jay? Margaret conceded that Maggie may have been seeing Phil Mitchell, Tom Carpenter and Jim Downey. She was relatively certain that Jay knew about Tom and Jim. Maggie had dated Jim in high school and still had strong feelings for him; in fact, the two had remained friends. Maggie had shared with Margaret that if things had been different in the last year of school, Maggie would have married Jim.

Did Margaret and Maggie get along? Margaret said that they did. They did have arguments from time to time, but nothing major. It was usually about Margaret's smoking or the one time she had let her sister, Emily, use Maggie's bed without consulting with her.

While the officers conferred, Jay and Margaret were left alone. Margaret's thoughts were about the murder of her roommate. Jay's concern was work. He made a comment to her that he was worried about being late for work. Margaret was angered by his apparent lack of compassion. "If that's all you can talk about, just be quiet," she snapped. At that moment, Margaret began to fearfully consider that Jay Carter may have had something to do with Maggie's death.

Detective Tolf told them that he would follow up with both of them with additional questions. For a short time, they went to the Hume house, a home thrown into the horror and chaos of a close-knit family in mourning.

Margaret called Jay's landlord, Russ Smith, and his wife, Stacey, as they were finishing dinner. Margaret told Stacey that she had some terrible news, "awful news about Maggie," and that her and Jay would be over shortly. At about 7:00 p.m., Jay and Margaret arrived. Margaret could not hold back: "You're not going to believe this, but Maggie was killed." Stacey remembered that Jay seemed upset as the two retold the story of what had happened to Maggie. Jay told her that he couldn't believe it had happened. "If it had been a car accident or cancer, he could have accepted it, but this…he just couldn't understand," Stacey said.

Jay related how he and John had searched the apartment. He told Stacey that he had opened the closet and saw a Snuggle Sack on the floor and just figured that Maggie had some laundry piled there. Jay also told her that he had noticed her glasses on the bedside table and thought that was strange. Jay told Stacey that he had been at Maggie's house the night before and that there had been a mysterious telephone call. Jay said that it was a black person calling and that when Maggie got the call, she made a strange face and hung up. He added that Maggie had gotten these calls before—something that he had not shared with the police only a few hours earlier.

Jay didn't go back to his apartment that night. Instead, he went to see his good friend and co-worker Terry Sheerer. Terry lived with another Beer Company employee, Kevin Danielson*. While Terry and Jay were close friends, Kevin had only known Jay a short time. When Jay conveyed the story of his last night with Maggie, how she had been receiving prank calls from a man, Kevin opted to leave and spend the night with someone else. This was not a matter that Kevin wanted to get involved with. He did remember wondering how a man, someone's fiancé, could leave his girlfriend alone at night when she was afraid and getting prank phone calls, especially when her roommate was not there. To Kevin, it struck him as an odd reaction for a man in Jay's position. Why hadn't he spent the night with Maggie?

Officers found Leigh Wilson, the woman Maggie had spent time with after work. Leigh indicated that Maggie had come over after stopping by her (Maggie's) parents' house. The two girls had hung out for a while. Then, at 8:15 p.m., they drove past Jay's apartment to see if he was home. He wasn't. Maggie then asked if Leigh would accompany her back to Dr. Chadwick's office. She needed to meet with Tom Carpenter about his termination.

The situation with Tom Carpenter was uncomfortable. Tom worked part time at Dr. Chadwick's office and was going to be fired the following morning. Maggie was going to be taking on his custodial responsibilities. While Maggie had informed Leigh of Tom's plight, Tom was unaware that Maggie would be replacing him—he only knew that Dr. Chadwick planned on letting him go in the morning. It was not a confrontational meeting, but it was certainly not upbeat. They had remained with Tom until about 9:30 p.m. For a while, the two girls drove around Battle Creek, talking. Maggie stopped at Leigh's. Leigh loaned Maggie a sweater. She had tried to call Maggie that night between 11:00 and 11:30 p.m., but the line had been busy.

The discussion with Leigh Wilson filled out most of Maggie's last evening when combined with the account given by Jay. At this stage of the investigation, however, it did not point to a clear suspect in the crime.

The canvassing of the neighbors in Maggie's apartment building offered some interesting and useful information. In the apartment under Maggie and Margaret's was Steven Ronning. Ronning had been paralyzed in a swimming accident. His brother, Michael, lived with him, but Michael was already packed with a full trailer, preparing to move to Texas. As an invalid, Ronning knew very little of the neighbors who lived on top of him and hadn't heard anything out of the ordinary the previous night.

Nineteen-year-old Shelly O'Neal, who lived in the building, said that she had heard of the homicide earlier that day. She and her boyfriend, Bob, both knew Maggie and knew that she was dating Jay. She usually knew when Jay came in because the front door of the apartment made a lot of noise. Bob had been at Shelly's apartment until 11:30 p.m. the night of the crime. When he left, Shelly looked out on the parking lot and waved goodbye to him. She didn't remember seeing Jay's car there, as it was usually parked in the street in front of the apartment. If someone had come in via the door while she was awake, she was sure that she would have heard it; that night, she hadn't heard anything.

Barbara and Isaiah Karim were the most promising witnesses of the tenants at 55 Stringham Road. Barbara said that she had been hearing voices for a period of three or four hours, on and off, coming from Maggie's apartment. At some point between 1:30 and 2:30 a.m. she was awakened by what she described as "a woman's scream." Barbara said that it was not a loud scream or anything that made her think that a person was calling for help, yet it had concerned her. She asked her husband if he had heard it, and he said that all he could hear were voices. Mrs. Karim said that she then went to her bedroom window and opened it. From there, she said that you could see a portion of the patio of apartment no. 19 from her bedroom window but not the door where you enter the apartment from the patio. Mrs. Karim told officers that during this time, she could hear voices coming from downstairs. She described one as being a male voice, due to the fact that it was quite low, and the other voice as being a female voice. She said that shortly after the scream, no more voices came from the apartment, but she heard movement. It could be that someone was walking around in the apartment. She said that she continued to keep her window cracked and that she definitely heard the patio door of apartment no. 19 either being opened or shut.

Her husband, Isaiah, had little to offer other than confirming the story that his wife had relayed. He also said that the girl killed was always fighting with her boyfriend. Their arguments had been far from quiet or infrequent.

Michael Griffin and his roommate, Scott Butcher, lived in apartment no. 17. Griffin had been at the movies with his brothers and returned late to the apartment—around the time that *M*A*S*H* was ending. When he pulled in, he noticed that the light was on in the living room of apartment no. 19. Griffin was laid off at the time, so he stayed up late watching Johnny Carson and then either David Letterman or David Snyder. The television was located against the wall that led to his roommate Scott's room, so he kept the volume very low. He had been up until about 1:30 to 2:00 a.m. and didn't hear anyone coming in or going out in the hallway outside. Griffin was sure that he would have heard anyone coming in or going out in the hallway due to the fact that the walls were so thin and he was deliberately keeping quiet so as to not disturb his roommate.

At about 11:00 p.m., Detectives VanStratton and Yesh arrived at the Leila Hospital morgue for a legal formality: the identification of the victim. Maggie's father, Michael, and Dr. Chadwick had come to the hospital and were joined by Dr. Cassin. It was a solemn moment as the sheet was pulled back; her father and employer confirmed that the remains were indeed of Maggie. Mike and Dr. Chadwick left.

Dr. Cassin's work was only beginning. At 12:59 a.m. in the quiet of the morgue, he began to perform the autopsy on Maggie Hume.

THE BOYFRIEND

You know I can't believe it when I hear that you won't see me
Don't. Don't you want me?
You know I don't believe you when you say that you don't need me
It's much too late to find
When you think you've changed your mind
You'd better change it back or we will both be sorry
                              —"Don't You Want Me," Human League

T he Battle Creek Police Department was faced with an almost herculean
    task even before the murder of Maggie Hume. The city it patrolled was
on the decline in the early 1980s, and with it came all of the problems and
crimes associated with such economic conditions.

   The world seemed to know Battle Creek from television. Anyone who
watched *Captain Kangaroo* or *The Beverley Hillbillies* knew that Battle Creek
was America's Cereal City. Saturday morning cartoons—back when they
were on television—were loaded with ads pushing sugar-coated grain in
some shape or form. The view the world had was one crafted by the ad
agencies and the image that corporations wanted to project. To watch
TV, you would have thought that Battle Creek had invented the concept
of breakfast.

   Battle Creek didn't create breakfast, but it did reinvent it. The city had
grown out of a skirmish between two Native Americans and a survey party in
1827. It was hardly a battle at all, although blood was drawn. The settlement

survived along the Territorial Road that ran east–west across the state. Battle Creek eventually became the "big city" of Calhoun County, Michigan.

The city became the headquarters for the Seventh-Day Adventist Church, and one of the best-known members, Dr. John Kellogg, established a sanitarium in the city. "The San," as it was referred to, was a health retreat for the rich and famous of the Victorian era. This was a hospital where they could detox and cleanse themselves, feasting on Dr. Kellogg's unique culinary concoctions. It was there, in the San, that Corn Flakes were created in 1898. Rice Krispies and an endless string of successful foods followed in the years after.

America used to eat breakfasts that more resembled dinners until the advent of breakfast cereals. One of the former San patients, Charles William (C.W.) Post, invented a cereal coffee (Postum), Grape-Nuts and Post Toasties in the same city. Post's factory was a mere block from the Kellogg Plant, making Battle Creek the hub of cereal production in the country. At one point, there were more than two dozen cereal or biscuit manufacturers in the city. On a given day, the citizens of the city and the surrounding countryside could tell you what was being made and in which plant simply by sniffing the air—so powerful was the sugary aroma that rose from the two plants.

Battle Creek was an industrial town in America's Rust Belt. There were businesses other than Post and the Kellogg Company, but the city thrived off the money that breakfast brought to the city. Where much of Michigan was tied to the auto industry, Battle Creek took pride in the fact that it served the world's first meal of the day. Train tracks snaked around and through the city, and most citizens padded at least fifteen minutes into any trip because you'd be stopped by a train trying to get into the downtown area. Its streets harkened back to an earlier era; made of red brick, they made your car seem to roar as it came into the city off the concrete paved roads.

Battle Creek boomed in the 1950s and '60s. In those decades, the downtown was a thriving business zone with two movie theaters, restaurants and even a high-end department store (Jacobson's). Big companies had offices downtown, including those of the old San, which was purchased by the federal government and brought in thousands of employees every day in its new guise, the Federal Center. Battle Creek seemed like it was on the cusp of becoming something bigger, something more, but it failed to reach that dream state.

The economic downturns of the 1970s brought grittier times to America's Cereal City. By the late 1970s and early 1980s, the culture and dynamics of the downtown were changing. Battle Creek and its nearby neighbor,

Kalamazoo, always shared an unspoken competition. In the 1970s, Kalamazoo had closed off its downtown main street to make an urban mall. At the same time, businesses in downtown Battle Creek were starting to suffer. Parking had always been challenging downtown, and people were willing to drive to Kalamazoo for its downtown and suburban malls for shopping. In 1974, one of Battle Creek's two downtown movie theaters, the Michigan Theater, closed its doors, cutting one of the key draws for people to come into the city for entertainment.

Battle Creek's response to Kalamazoo was to attempt to copy its idea of an urban mall. In 1975, Michigan Avenue, the main street, was closed off and replaced with planters, benches and bizarre sculptures. Parking lots were added. Downtown Battle Creek had become the Michigan Mall.

It was a concept that was flawed almost from the beginning. The businesses on the side streets were cut off from the mall shoppers and traffic and disappeared in a matter of just a few years. Instead of parking in front of the business at which you wanted to shop, you had to park blocks away and walk, sometimes in the snow, to an outdoor mall setting. The Veteran's Hospital thought that it was a progressive idea to run a bus shuttle to the Michigan Mall to drop off vets with their government checks, but this resulted in drinking, a rise in prostitution and other problems associated with individuals who had physical or mental problems being turned loose in the heart of a city.

A spike in urban crime didn't help matters either. Battle Creek had always had a division between black and white residents, as well as strained racial relationships. The mall seemed to draw the worst of both races. Long before the phrase "flash robbery," gangs of kids would invade and rob a downtown business in a matter of moments before moving on. Businesses downtown called one another to warn of groups of kids swarming the mall looking for trouble, often giving them time to lock up before the gangs arrived. People no longer felt comfortable going downtown to Battle Creek to shop. The Michigan Mall had not saved downtown Battle Creek; it came close to killing it.

Downtown Battle Creek suffered another blow when plans were announced to build a more traditional mall outside the city limits. The year 1982 marked the start of construction on the Lakeview Square Mall, miles outside the city. It was new, clean, free of the inner-city crime problems and drew even more people away from the heart of the city. Even the promise of the Kellogg Company to build its new world headquarters downtown in 1981 did not seem to introduce hope of reviving the downtown economy. Kellogg's, which had always been friendly with the community, was suddenly holding Battle Creek hostage, demanding that Battle Creek Township and the city merge or it would build its headquarters elsewhere. Voters, more out of fear than anything else, agreed to the merger, but it left a bitter taste in everyone's mouth.

The Battle Creek Police Department struggled with this change of culture and subsequent rise of crime. In the first half of the 1980s, Calhoun County averaged only 1 to 3 murders per year. Michigan as a whole had 872 homicides in the year that Maggie Hume had been murdered. Drugs like cocaine, which seemed like a "big city" problem, penetrated Battle Creek too. Drugs brought in gangs, and gangs brought violence and other crimes. The police had to struggle against these changes while, at the same time, the tax base for the downtown area plummeted, with businesses fleeing the failed Michigan Mall. It created a pressure cooker for officers and their leaders— not the best environment for a complicated murder like Maggie Hume's.

ON AUGUST 19, DETECTIVE TOLF was visited by Tom Carpenter, who had worked with Maggie up until the day she didn't show up for work. Carpenter was a short, fit, light-haired graduate of Harper Creek High School in 1980. In 1982, to pay for school at KCC, he worked at a pizza parlor in town and was a custodial engineer at Dr. Chadwick's office, where Maggie worked. His tasks were mundane, usually coming in the early morning to clean the office. Before working at the doctor's office, he had never met Maggie, although they did have a mutual friend, Ginger Martin.

Tom first met Maggie when he went in to pick up his paycheck. The two were not friends but were on a friendly basis. Tom was sure that Dr. Chadwick was planning on firing him. He didn't hold the doctor in good stead—he felt he was condescending. The night that Maggie died, he had confided to her his feelings, and she told him that he would not be fired, assuring him that his job was secure. Since the Humes were friendly with Dr. Chadwick, Tom assumed that Maggie had some sort of inside track and felt comfortable opening up with her. He described her as "happy-go-lucky."

The morning that Maggie didn't show up at work, Tom did. He was told by Dr. Chadwick that he was going to be let go and that Maggie, the person who had reassured him that his job was safe, was going to be taking over his responsibilities. Tom was stunned by the announcement, and given the way that Dr. Chadwick had stated it, the responsibility for letting him go should have been Maggie's.

He left Dr. Chadwick's office upset. Maggie, he felt, had played him for a fool. He was not upset at having lost the job; "whatever" had been his response. He was only slightly upset that Maggie had pretended to be friendly to him when, in reality, she knew all along that he was going to be fired. At the same time, Tom didn't like Dr. Chadwick, so his departure was no reason to get angry.

The night of August 18, Tom's father called him at the pizza parlor where he worked and told him that Maggie Hume had been killed. Almost instantly, his frustration with Maggie turned to compassion. "Poor Maggie," was what a saddened Tom said to Detective Tolf.

Tom Carpenter had never dated Maggie. He had only gotten to know her the last few weeks of her life. He was seeing someone else at the time. The loss of one of his minimum-wage jobs was hardly enough to send him into a murderous rage. Police marked off Tom Carpenter as having anything to do with Maggie's demise.

Dr. Cassin completed his preliminary autopsy report. At five single-spaced pages, it was a comprehensive report on what Maggie had endured the last few minutes of her life. Like most autopsy reports, it is cold and factual. "Death is attributed to cerebral amoxia produced by ligature strangulation." A distinct half-inch horizontal hemorrhage was noted on her neck where someone had used something to strangle her.

There was more. Maggie had been raped—sodomized by her attacker. The last few minutes of her life had been exceedingly violent, perpetrated by someone who maintained dominance over her until the end. There were no other marks on her face or neck other than the ligature pattern. It was impossible to tell what had been used to strangle her in the attack.

There were other materials recovered. Her underpants had secretions that were consistent with semen and were sent out for testing. Hairs were found on her neck and from her side, but the assumption was that they were from Maggie. Several fibers were found on her bedsheet that were consistent with the red carpet in the apartment. Police never released any of the details from the report to the press.

One of the key interviews that Detective Pestun led was conducted with Jim Downey, Maggie's former boyfriend. Jay had named Jim as one of the people who might have wanted to harm Maggie. Jim had known Maggie from his freshman year in high school. They had dated near the end of their senior year. Their relationship had been intimate and almost like something scripted out of a 1980s teen love movie. The two of them had been intimate once or twice at his parents' house. After breaking up, they remained good friends. Jim had even helped Maggie move into her apartment.

Jim had left Battle Creek for military school for a year. He then came back to Battle Creek, working as a security guard at Union Pump. He had started dating another young woman, Theresa Burkhart, and the two of them were engaged to be married. On the night of the murder, the two of them had been at the Calhoun County Fair in Marshall. Jim had returned to his parents' home on Winter Street but had no solid alibi, as his parents were at their cottage at the time. His brother, David, may have been at home, but he wasn't sure.

When he returned to his place, he called Maggie's apartment. Maggie had asked him to secure some beer for her roommate's upcoming birthday party. When he called at 10:30 p.m., Downey heard a television on in the background. He told her who it was, but Maggie didn't respond to him other than to hang up. Jim tried to call her again, several times, at about 11:30 p.m., but the line was busy.

Detectives Tolf and Pestun had heard rumors that Jim Downey had accessed Maggie's apartment via the balcony before. Given that the murderer had done the same, it was the kind of detail that drew their scrutiny. Jim retold the story. At the beginning of the summer of 1982, he and some friends had been playing a practical joke on her roommate, Margaret. Jim said he, Mike Beck and Mark Thomas wanted to startle Margaret. Mark and Mike lifted Jim onto the balcony; Jim knocked on door. The door was locked, but he had surprised Margaret, who let him in and let the other two young men in via the front door. Margaret was not alone at the time; her sister and a group of four friends were over.

The detectives pressed Jim on his relationship with Maggie, but according to Jim, they had simply remained friends. He admitted that he had heard a rumor that Maggie had an abortion in 1981, during the time when they were still dating. Maggie had confided to him later that she had indeed undertaken the alleged procedure in Grand Rapids and that she had not told her parents at that time. Jim admitted that it bothered him that she had done this without consulting with him.

When the police pressed him as to who he thought might have killed Maggie, at first he said no one crossed his mind. "I can't think of why anyone would want to kill Maggie." When pressed further, he did say that he felt her boyfriend Jay may have done it. "I don't know why," he said. Maggie had told him that she and Jay were going to be getting married. Things were not always smooth between the two of them though. "Not that long ago, Maggie and Jay had broken up for about a week," but the two of them had gotten back together after that.

There were rumors circulating that Jim had been seeing Maggie recently, but he denied them. The two of them had been friends, that much was true, but nothing more than that. Jim maintained steadfastly that he had been loyal to his fiancée, Theresa. At no point had Maggie given him any indication that she wanted to rekindle their former relationship.

When the detectives asked Jim if he was willing to provide hair, fingerprint and blood samples, he agreed. He also willingly undertook two polygraph tests. The first one had come back with some inconclusive responses, but on the second one, Jim had passed with flying colors. He had been over to the Hume house the night her body had been found to offer his condolences and be there to support them.

To the detectives, Jim Downey was merely a good friend of Maggie's, with no tangible reason to want her dead.

MEANWHILE, AT THE HUME HOUSE, family and friends began to assemble. Jay's activities during this period caught the attention of the people there. The evening when Maggie's body had been discovered, Wednesday, August 18, Jay had visited the Hume household for only an hour or so. When Mrs. Hume inquired as to where Jay was, he had told family members that he had to go to work. He returned after work for a short time, not mingling with the Hume family but with Maggie's circle of friends. The small gang of kids assembled on the curb outside the Hume home, talking, included Phil Mitchell, Jay Carter, Lynn Van Geison and Mary Landstra. Phil had dated Maggie for some time, and Mary was one of Maggie's oldest friends. Jay told them how he and John Hume had gone to the apartment and had found Maggie's glasses on the nightstand in her room. According to Jay, the finding of the glasses had triggered them going to the police. The officers had returned to the apartment and had found her body in the closet.

Jay conveyed that Maggie had been raped. Phil and Jay entered into a juvenile description of what they would do with the guy who had done this to Maggie. They were going to tie him up and castrate him. Jay described cutting off this murderer's fingers and toes—essentially torturing her killer. At this time, however, authorities had not told anyone of Maggie's rape, especially someone they considered a potential suspect.

What none of the young men and women knew was that Mrs. Hume was lying on her bed listening to their discussion. Jay once more seemed to reiterate that Maggie had been raped. In her words, they talked about stringing the killer up by his thumbs.

Virgil Jay Carter, Maggie's then boyfriend and the prime suspect. *Courtesy of the LaPorte County Historical Society.*

On Thursday, as the house filled with supporters, Jay didn't arrive until the late afternoon. He sat opposite of Mrs. Hume, wringing his hands and staring as if to avoid eye contact with her. When she pressed him into conversation, Jay began to talk nervously. Jay indicated, more than once, that he knew her death was an accident. He said that he knew that the killer cared about her because he had wrapped and covered her so neatly and carefully with a Snuggle Sack. Jay also told Mrs. Hume that he knew that Maggie had been raped, something he conveyed to her more than once.

Jay revealed that her wallet and a flight bag with albums were missing. He indicated that her purse was "outside." In a strange attempt to reassure Mrs. Hume, Jay told her that Maggie must have known who her killer was because the apartment was not broken into. He also told her that Maggie had been in her nightgown, ready for bed. Many of these details Jay said more than once.

Lorie Hume was taken aback. Jay seemed to know more about the death of her daughter than the Hume family knew at the time. It struck her as odd that the police would have shared these details of the crime scene with Jay before they had told the Humes. At the Hume home, Jay spoke with Susan Schuitema, Maggie's cousin. He told her that Maggie's room was messier than normal. Maggie had a lock on the bedroom door, and according to Jay, if she had locked it, her death might have been avoided.

Susan had gotten very little from Mike Hume about the crime, mostly because the family had not been told much. Jay seemed to have a wealth of information, though. She asked him how someone had gotten into the apartment. She had heard that there was no sign of forced entry. Jay responded, "Oh yeah, the balcony the lock on the balcony was picked." He went on to tell her that the apartment had not been ransacked but that Maggie's bed had been torn apart.

The next day, in a separate conversation, Jay went into more detail with Susan. He reiterated that Maggie had a cold that night. When he and John had gone to look for Maggie, Jay checked the closet to look for her clothes. He was familiar with what she wore and was hoping to identify what she might be wearing. Jay said that while searching the bedroom, he noticed the sleeping bag on the floor but didn't think much of it. He said he wasn't looking for "a dead Maggie" but was simply trying to find out what clothes she might be wearing.

According to Jay, the killer put her, "nice and neat," in a Snuggle Sack, with her head to the side and clothes put on top of her. He added a grisly detail. According to what he told Ms. Schuitema, her body had left an imprint on the floor of the closet. Jay added that he and Maggie were going to be engaged at Christmas.

Phyllis Hume, Maggie's aunt, caught some of the conversation as well. "The person who killed Maggie didn't mean to do it, and [Jay] said they found Maggie neatly placed in a snug sack, with her head turned to the side." Her recollection was that Jay had said that Maggie had put on a green shorty nightgown, and when he was looking in the closet, with John Hume peering over his shoulder, he thought that he saw the green nightgown on a pile of clothes on the floor. He went on to say that the Snug Sack wasn't in its normal place, but he didn't think anything of it.

Jay's presence at the Hume home was not one of a supportive person. He was in and out constantly, gone sometimes for hours at a time. When he was present, he seemed nervous. While the community provided an outpouring of sympathy, Mrs. Hume struggled with the tasks necessary for her daughter's funeral. Maggie would need clothing to be buried in, which meant a trip to the apartment and the scene of the crime. Mrs. Hume asked Jay to come along with her, along with her sister, Cindy Gillett; John Hume; and her husband, Mike.

Jay hung back in the doorway, reluctant to join in. Mrs. Hume was looking for something with a high collar to conceal the marks on her daughter's neck but struggled with a selection since most of Maggie's clothing was low cut. Ultimately she opted for a long blouse in St. Phil's school colors and white pants. As she looked for accessories, Jay came into the bedroom and mentioned that Maggie never took off her diamond ring and that he knew it was in the drawer of her dresser. He went over, and under her underwear was the ring, wrapped in wax paper. It wasn't until later that Mrs. Hume began to wonder just how Jay knew exactly where the ring was if she wore it constantly.

The family gathered things like her photo album, her purse, a book, some other clothing and her glasses. Cindy documented what was removed for the police. Mrs. Hume was unsure what belt to take so she took two of them. As she chose, she looked over, and Jay was chewing his fingernails.

When the Hume family got home, they discovered that Maggie's checkbook, which was presumed to have been stolen, was in a pocket of her purse. Apparently the police had overlooked it during their investigation at the crime scene.

Jay had told the family that Maggie had smelled smoke, presumably from oil, in her car the night of her murder. The Humes drove the green Hornet over to their friends, the Landstras. They had the car for several days in their garage, and there was no sign of oil leaking at all or the mysterious odor.

Jay told Mrs. Hume that he was having a hard time getting in contact with his parents for the funeral. He used this as an excuse to leave, despite the fact that Mrs. Hume told him that he was welcome to use their telephone. By Friday, the Landstras had asked him if he had managed to get ahold of his parents, and he responded that he would do it later. Jay left often, something that was not lost on the Humes. At Maggie's Rosary, several people noticed that he kept turning around and fidgeting, looking as if he wanted to be somewhere else.

Jay had reasons for being nervous. The police were bringing him in to interview with different officers, each attempting to wrap their heads around the story that Jay told. His story was different at each recounting. On August 22, he interviewed with Detective Dennis Mullen. He told Mullen that he could only stay at Maggie's for one to two hours, but later he said that he could only stay for an hour. He hinted that Maggie may have been asking him if he was planning on spending the night because she was, perhaps, expecting someone else that evening.

Detective Alan Tolf got his chance to interview Jay on August 25. Tolf joined the Battle Creek Police Department in 1967, having been born and raised in Battle Creek. Homicides were something with which he had a lot of experience. "I knew at the age of ten I wanted to be a detective. I was promoted to detective after four and a half years; it broke the rules at the time. This wasn't a job for me; it was a way of life. I read everything I could find about investigations, interrogation techniques." Tolf was a cop's cop, tough and smart, and he saw Jay Carter as the only possible suspect in the case. Even today, he concedes that mistakes were made in how Jay was handled. "[Pestun] should have got him that day [of the murder] and held him. That's what I would have done. It's not classic how it was handled."

Tolf was like a pit bull in his persistence. "I was interviewing him, and I was totally convinced of his guilt. We used to do interrogations for hours and hours at a time, to wear somebody down. I had him in there. He started by folding his arms, hung his head low. I told him things like, 'Look, it's down to you and me. There are no other suspects other than you. I understand, it was probably an accident, but you need to come clean with us.'"

For his part, Jay started to wither under the pressure. He made comments like, "It was probably an accident. She was probably killed by somebody that she knew." He conceded that Maggie had probably been killed in her bed. He even said that her wallet had likely been taken to make it look like a robbery. He told the detective that they had made love in the living room with the blinds open, which seemed contrary to Maggie's conservative character. For Tolf, these were all strong hints that Jay knew more than he was letting on about the murder. Unrelenting, Tolf told Jay that as far as he was concerned, Jay had killed his girlfriend. "He was breaking."

"When I was interrogating Jay, I asked him, 'What do you think is going to happen to you today?' He said, 'You're going to lock me up.' Innocent guys don't say that during interrogations. They say things like, 'I'll stay here all day. I'm innocent—nothing is going to happen to me!' Not Jay. That says a lot right there."

Suddenly, Battle Creek police chief Thomas Thear entered the room. The chief had been watching from behind the two-way mirror in the next room. He shattered the deliberate tension in the room with the order, "Put him on the polygraph right away."

According to Detective Tolf, "Well, that broke it up. I called the Kalamazoo Police Department, and they said to send him home, then bring him down at about 6:00 p.m. So I sent him home. What I didn't know was that night, the *Enquirer and News* had a headline that 'Police Have No Suspects in the Hume Case'…or something like that. Well, when I picked him up, he was a different person—belligerent, outright antagonistic." Tolf conceded that you only get one chance at breaking a potential suspect, and the interruption by the police chief had taken that moment away from him and had given Jay a chance to regain his composure.

The polygraph session did not go well for Jay, though. Detective Hanechow led the session and confronted him with a battery of questions. Jay, for his part, was hostile during the session. During one of his previous interviews, Jay had told Patrolman Brenner that when he had been at Maggie's apartment with John Hume, he had been looking for Maggie's shoes. At first he denied having looked into the closet at all. Then he denied that he had been looking for her shoes. His story was highly inconsistent and varied with each telling.

The police asked him if he had walked across the grass at the apartment complex. "I walked across the grass, could have, but would have been gone going up carpet steps." When faced with the key questions regarding his involvement in Maggie's death, Jay failed the polygraph.

Most seasoned inspectors will tell you, if you ask, that you can't beat the polygraph, but you can beat the operator. The machine measures physical reactions to questions. Everything depends on the questions that are being asked. Polygraphs are inadmissible in court because of this, but they do allow investigators to see when someone is being deceptive so that they can concentrate their investigations. In some cases, they are used to compel people to confess, knowing that the machine will catch them. This wasn't the case with Jay Carter. He didn't confess, but his answers were clearly showing that he was not being truthful.

Jay responded to a large number of questions. He made the statement that the killer probably thought "if I can't have her, nobody can." Jay also told Detective Hanechow that when he had been in her bedroom prior to the body being found, he had been in the closet looking for her shoes.

According to Detective Tolf, "We got into his interrogation and he jerked off all of the probes and said, 'I don't have to take this!'" The officers took notes that night, capturing several key bits of information gleaned from Jay. Their notes indicated:

- *Suspect has extremely strong ego*
- *Never uses the word "love" in describing his feelings for the victim, family, or friends*
- *Is a loner outside of his association with the victim, both at work and not.*
- *Appears to be a "penny-pincher"*
- *Admits relationship with the victim was a "convenient" one because:*
    - *~ made sure he would eat*
    - *~ companion*
    - *~ sex pleasures*
    - *~ helped keep his clothes clean*
- *Shows little emotion over the death of the victim*
- *Strongly claims that the victim "was my whole life"*
- *Has good control over emotions while being questioned. He could not be angered, yet, claims to have a bad temper*
- *Has an answer or explanation for almost every question asked*
- *Has no alibi for whereabouts that evening and early morning of 8-17 and 8-18*
- *Seems to possess knowledge of interrogation techniques*
- *Is aware that we have no hard, physical evidence against him, and no witnesses*
- *Would be logical suspect for taking purse* [wallet] *and records from victim*
- *Only person that knew that roommate would be delayed in coming home the night of offense*
- *Only person who would hide body to buy time, knowing that the roommate would check the victim upon arrival home (between 3:30 and 4:00 a.m.)*
- *Motive would be the fear that he was losing victim in relationship (ego)*
- *Made the statement that the killer probably had thought that "if I can't have her, nobody can"*

Jay was asked if he would provide a sample of his blood and hair for testing against the evidence. He consented, but because he left in such a hurry the samples were not obtained. To the officers tied to the case, it appeared that there was only one primary suspect. They let Jay Carter know that it was him and that he had failed his polygraph examination.

DARK SUSPICIONS

Now, could I have loved someone like the one I see in you
Yeah, I remember the good times baby now, and the bad times too
These last few weeks of holding on
The days are dull, the nights are long
Guess it's better to say
Goodbye to you

—*"Goodbye to You," Scandal*

Jay Carter's behavior with the Humes did not seem to improve after his failed polygraph examination. On the day after his exam, August 26, he arrived at the Hume household and informed Maggie's mother, Lorie, that he had failed his testing and that police had told him he was the prime suspect. He left after a short while claiming that he needed to get a lawyer. Later, he returned and handed over several albums of Maggie's that he had. Jay didn't come into the house. Mrs. Hume was blunt with him: She told him that if he was innocent, he needed to cooperate with the police. If not, he needed to confess and get it over with. Jay gave no answer to her. He simply left.

The Landstra family, close friends with the Hume family, were loaning their home adjacent to the Humes to accommodate the extended Hume family that was coming into Battle Creek to help them in their time of mourning. The Landstras were staying with friends of theirs when one of Maggie's closest friends, Mary, received two to three telephone calls from Jay in the week that followed her friend's death. "I don't know how, but Jay somehow got the number and called me there. He said he needed to talk.

He wanted to know if I would go to the movies with him. I told him no. He called a few times, asking me to go out with him for dinner." According to the police reports, he had told her, "We're both going through the same thing." Maggie's funeral had not even taken place, and Jay was asking one of Maggie's friends on a date—suspicious behavior in the eyes of police.

As Mary retold the story thirty-two years later, "The police met with me once with my parents, and I told them about it. The police looked to my mother and said, 'Don't let her go out with him.' That really told me something."

Maggie's funeral was on Saturday August 21, 1982, and was largely attended. Reverend Fitzgerald presided over the service at St. Philip Catholic Church, which had played such an important role in her life. Not only did she have a large family and considerable number of friends, but her father's popularity also brought in many who wanted to offer the Hume family support. She was laid to rest at Memorial Park Cemetery.

Even at the funeral, Jay's interactions with the mourners seemed out of place. At the graveside service, Jay was acting nervous. He approached one of Maggie's friends whom he knew, Lynn Van Geison, and hugged her. "You know Maggie is my world," he said.

It struck Lynn as odd. She had not talked to Jay in a long time, and his behavior struck her as "suspicious." Jay went on to let Lynn know that he was a suspect in Maggie's death and told her, "My conscience is clear," a statement he repeated several times in the short conversation. Lynn snapped at him, "Calm down. Why are you thinking about that right now?" From that point on, he avoided direct eye contact with her. Lynn, to her credit, didn't hold back. She asked Jay flat out if he had killed Maggie. He denied it: "How could you think I'd do that?"

Apparently Lynn's question had some merit behind it. On August 30, police received a tip from St. Phil's volleyball coach, Sheila Guerra. On February 10, 1982, Jay had an altercation at a St. Phil volleyball game with Maggie that had been witnessed by Mrs. Guerra and several students. Mrs. Guerra knew both Maggie and Jay personally, and the incident stuck in her mind quite vividly. According to her, Jay was choking Maggie with his hands when he was confronted by her and several students. Jay made the comment to her, "I will choke the life out of her and hide her where no one could find her." The comments, in light of the crime and the method of Maggie's death, struck investigators as no small coincidence.

Two additional students who witnessed the event were tracked down, Michael Porter and his sister, Sara. At the time, both confirmed that the incident took place. While they did not know Maggie personally, they knew who she was. Michael Porter was interviewed in detail about the incident in 2000 and recalled it this way: "Uh, yes we went outside of the, uh, basketball or volleyball court, out where the trophy cases and the hallways; there was, uh, like a fight going on, and it was first he was choking her at the front and she was struggling. And he got behind her and was choking her, and her glasses weren't on you could see, but I could see that she was very scared. Um, Mrs. Guerra came out with and there was a few other people uh my sister was there and what had happened was uh Mrs. Guerra got him off her, and uh then the comment was in there about that I remember still today where he made a threat of what he was going to do with her. I remember hearing him making the threat of what he was going to do with her, uh, he was going to kill her."

His sister Sara's recollection was equally disturbing. She remembered Jay yelling at Maggie, saying that he "was going to put her in a dark place where nobody would find her."

At the time, no one thought much of the incident. But when considered with the circumstances of Maggie's death, it seemed to investigators to have been a premonition of the horror to come. Suspecting that Jay might claim that he was at work at the time of the game, the officers went to the Beer Company and pulled his timecard for the night of the volleyball game in question. Jay had punched out at 8:30 p.m., which would have given him plenty of time to attend the nighttime game.

One might try and argue that perhaps Sheila Guerra had misidentified Jay as the man choking Maggie, but Jay had begun visiting Mrs. Guerra after the funeral. In an interview with police on September 1, 1982, Mrs. Guerra conveyed the details of what Jay had been telling her in their visits. His version of events did not waver much from what he had said previously— that he had waited at Maggie's apartment for a few minutes, went to the Ritzee, checked her car for problems and so on. He did tell Mrs. Guerra that Maggie had been killed in her bed and that "it was an accident." As he had done with the Humes, he told her that Maggie had been raped as well. He admitted that he had been listening in on the phone call that Jim Downey had made when Jim had called Maggie—a new detail that he had omitted in conversation with the police.

Just the day before, another member of the tight-knit St. Phil community, Linda Albrecht, had reached out to investigators concerning conversations that she had been having with Jay. Mrs. Albrecht was the mother of a volleyball player at St. Phil and considered herself to be good friends with both Maggie and Jay. Jay had visited her house several times since the murder and confided in her. As with Sheila Guerra, he retold his version of events. Jay added the detail that when he had left her apartment, Maggie's bed had been made. Jay opened up to her, saying, "I don't have anybody here now." He thought that Maggie would feel okay if he became friends with Mrs. Albrecht. Jay's timeline of events restated that he and Maggie had sex prior to the first telephone call coming into the apartment.

On Monday, August 30, Jay showed up at Linda Albrecht's home, surprising her since she didn't know that he knew where she lived. At one point, she openly stated to Jay that "there was a possibility that she knew how it [the murder] had happened." Jay became very rigid and looked at her strangely. "You don't really think I did it do you?" He then broke down and cried. He told her how he planned to share the rest of his life with Maggie and have kids.

Linda Albrecht came close to the point with him: "Did the police department check your body?" Jay became somewhat surprised and said, "No, why would they do that?"

The rumor mill around Battle Creek often traveled faster than reality. A rumor had sprung up that someone had been arrested in Maggie's murder. Linda Albrecht contacted Jay by phone and passed on the rumor to him. "You got to be kidding. Good, now I'm off the hook," he said.

Both Sheila Guerra and Linda Albrecht confided to the police that there was no doubt in their minds that Jay had killed Maggie. Linda went so far as to offer to coddle up to Jay. Given her age and his, he might identify with her as a mother figure and eventually confess.

The investigators kept their focus on Jay Carter. Detective Pestun traveled down to Westville, Indiana, where Jay was from, to try and get some background information on him. In some respects, he didn't come across anything tangible in his background. Jay had not gotten any tickets in his hometown. He had dated one steady girlfriend while in high school, but she had moved out of state with her family and was unavailable for interviewing.

At Jay's high school, the majority of teachers (and the principal) who knew him had left for other jobs. One who remained, Mr. Fagg, was able to provide some background on Jay, who had graduated in 1978 with an average GPA. According to Mr. Fagg, Jay had tried to become a honor student but was unable to meet the requirements. Once he learned that he couldn't join the program, he became critical of it.

While Jay played basketball, it was clear that his true love was volleyball. He proved to be highly competitive. Jay was the kind of person who expected everyone to equal his ability when it came to volleyball. He expected perfection from his teammates and became upset when someone made a mistake. When it came to his own mistakes, Jay was always able to provide an explanation for his errors.

From what Detective Pestun could gather from his interviews in Indiana, Jay was very demanding on his parents. He always wanted the new thing, shoes, clothing and so on. He demanded a new van, and his parents indulged him. His parents were not made of money. They had asked to purchase his graduation announcements on credit.

As Mr. Fagg put it, "He was a fringe nonconformist; he was critical of things he didn't agree with or things he could not do. [He] had the attitude of my way or it's not right."

ON OCTOBER 2, MAGGIE'S full autopsy report was finally completed. Her death had been from strangulation via a ligature. Maggie had suffered two wounds to her head, both of which had occurred while she was still alive. Her attacker had sodomized her, and that attack had taken place while she had been alive as well. There were signs that she struggled with her killer in an effort to avoid the rape. Whoever had attacked Maggie had been very athletic and physically strong.

The release of the autopsy report in October was the first acknowledgement from authorities that Maggie had been raped. Even then, police held back on the information that was provided to the press. For example, they acknowledged that Maggie had been strangled, but the ligature was never mentioned. At no point did the press release any information on the position of the body in the closet, how the killer entered the apartment and so on. These would be facts that would be crucial later in the investigation.

With the release of the autopsy report, a full understanding of what took place the night Maggie died began to unfold. Maggie had most likely gone to bed, based on the fact that when her brother and Jay had come into the apartment during their failed search, her alarm clock was going off. Most people set their alarm clocks just before going to sleep. It is highly probable that her attacker surprised her in her bedroom after she had gone to bed.

Based on the testimony of her roommate, Margaret, and Jay, the apartment was locked at the time of the attack. Thomas Strong, one of River Apartment's maintenance men, said that he had cut the grass the day of her death. This was important because the grass clippings were found as a trail in the apartment. Maggie's killer had climbed up to the balcony and had entered through the doorway. Based on the grass clippings, the murderer went only to Maggie's bedroom. It was there, possibly on the bed, that the

The hallway of Maggie and Margaret's apartment. The murderer went down this hall straight to Maggie's room. *Provided via FOIA, Battle Creek Police Department.*

struggle took place during which her life was taken. From the wounds on her head, her attacker had struck her there first, possibly knocking her glasses off and leaving Maggie all but blind to the assault she endured. Based on the screams heard by the neighbors, the attack most likely took place between 1:00 and 2:00 a.m. Her killer sodomized her and then strangled her with a belt or similar object.

Her killer did not immediately flee but instead took steps to attempt to cover up the crime. The murderer had taken her wallet out, most likely to

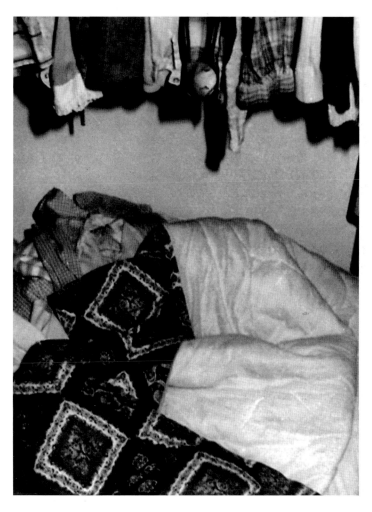

The Snuggle Sack in which Maggie was wrapped. Why would a murderer take the time to do this unless he knew for sure that her roommate was not coming home soon? *Provided via FOIA, Battle Creek Police Department.*

make it look like a robbery, with the purse ending up on the floor of the closet. The killer then positioned her body in the closet and took precious time to conceal her under the blanket and sleeping bag out of sight.

The concealment of the body could have been done for two reasons. One was to delay its finding so as to provide the killer distance (both time and physically) from the discovery so as to throw off suspicion. Another was that the covering of the body was done by someone who knew the victim—an act of guilt, an echo of caring after a savage and brutal assault.

Whoever entered the apartment did not go down the hall and into Margaret Van Winkle's bedroom, indicating that the killer knew that Maggie was alone—otherwise he or she would have checked to see if Margaret was present to avoid the risk of being discovered in the heinous act. The killer left via the balcony as well, so when Margaret came home, the door to the apartment was still locked from the inside.

To detectives working the case, Jay Carter still seemed the most likely person to have committed the crime. Detective Pestun fell back on a time-tested investigation tool: re-creation of the timeline. Many criminals, when they fabricate an alibi, fail to take into account the time their actions take. Going to the Beer Company where Jay worked, Pestun was able to check when Jay had clocked out of work. A check of the phone company's records pinpointed the exact time of the two known phone calls that came into the apartment that night: when Margaret had called Maggie to tell her that she was going to be late in coming back from the airport and when Jim Downey had called.

From this Pestun added in the elements of the story that Jay had provided. He went so far as to drive from the Beer Company on the route that Jay said he had taken and at the same time of day. The timeline that was laid out only seemed to add to the suspicion of Jay's version of events. Jay clocked out at work at 9:54 p.m. It took eight minutes to drive from his work to Maggie's apartment, where he discovered that she was not at home. He claimed to have waited there for a few minutes and then drove to the nearby Urbandale Ritzee, where he attempted to call Maggie, but she wasn't there. At best speed and traffic, this would have been 10:02 p.m. or later, depending on how long he waited at the apartment complex, according to Pestun's reckoning.

Maggie supposedly spotted Jay and pulled into the Ritzee, where they talked. According to Jay, she complained about an odor from her car. Jay checked her car there but could not find anything. He then claimed to have followed her to her apartment and checked her engine there. They then went up in the apartment. In the apartment, the two of them had intercourse, and Jay made soup—all by the time that the collect call from Margaret Van Winkle came in at 10:19 p.m., according to the telephone records. Piecing together Jay's story, he had accomplished a nearly impossible number of tasks in the timeframe that the call provided. For the investigators, this seemed to indicate that parts of Jay's story simply didn't add up.

Detective Dennis Mullen met with Jay on October 10, 1982, to once more attempt to clarify his story (or further define the holes in it). Mullen had been part of the Battle Creek Township Police, which had been merged into the Battle Creek City Police Department when Kellogg's had forced the mandate/vote on merging the two communities as part of its demands to keep its corporate headquarters in Battle Creek. Mullen had been a medic in Vietnam and had solid experience investigating murders in the city.

Mullen's interview with Jay highlighted some of the conflicts with his testimony. He blamed detectives for mixing up his account of events. Jay said that he did not check out Maggie's car at the Ritzee but rather looked at it at her apartment because it smelled of smoke, changing his story again. He did add that they spent several minutes at the Ritzee talking.

Jay told Detective Mullen that he would agree to talk to him one more time but "would not continue this." He wanted the police questioning to stop, as he "knows I am not involved." Jay told Mullen that he did not want to go through the hassle of explaining himself and repeating himself for years to come. "I have nothing to prove."

Jay asked Mullen what he knew about the case and whether he could help him solve the crime. Mullen responded that he simply wanted to know what Jay knew. As Jay retold his story, Mullen was able to glean a few additional details out of him. Jay said that he and Maggie only had sex to make him happy—that she did not enjoy it that much. He added, however, that this time she may have wanted it.

Jay told Mullen that Maggie had not told him that she had received any prank phone calls. He repeated that he had gotten her a blanket because she was cold and that he walked her into her bedroom and got her a birth control pill from the top of the dresser.

Jay then mentioned that he needed to leave the interview to get to work. When Mullen asked him if he wanted to talk again, Jay said that he wanted to "get over it" and that it would take him some time to get over it all. With the time constraints, Mullen broached the contradictions and issues with Jay's comments.

First up, he referenced the remarks that Mrs. Hume had raised that Maggie had been raped. Jay denied making those comments the day that

Mrs. Hume claimed. He did add that he may have later said that Maggie had been raped. He denied any knowledge that Maggie had been raped prior to the public announcement. Jay went on to say that he never said that "whoever did this must have loved her" or that her death had been "an accident." Mrs. Hume had simply been wrong.

Jay ended the interview with Mullen by stating that he was a firm believer in God, although he did not go to church. He claimed that he had changed his lifestyle somewhat since the murder and that God had punished him by taking Maggie away from him for the "lifestyle" that he had lived.

On October 25, more than a month after the murder, officers contacted Jay to obtain his blood, hair and saliva samples, which he had agreed to provide at the time of his polygraph. Jay's response was, "I'll have to think about it," with no commitment. Such samples would likely prove to be of little use. Jay admitted to being in the apartment. He admitted as well to having sex with Maggie the night of her murder. This was an age before DNA testing, and even with it, all it would do was validate Jay's account. His refusal to provide the samples didn't seem like the actions of a fiancé wanting to clear his name or assist with the investigation.

Two days later, a warrant was issued for Jay to provide the samples. Detective Mary Lou Zuiderveen was sent to pick him up at the Beer Company and obtain his biological samples. Zuiderveen was a trailblazer in the Battle Creek Police Department. She had joined the force in 1972 and was not even allowed to ride with male officers because of the "scandal" it might cause. In 1981, Chief Thear had told her she would have to test for her position just to keep it; she not only passed but was also first on the promotional list for detective—Battle Creek's first.

Detective Zuiderveen reached out to one of Maggie's close friends, Mary Beth Landstra, to see what the relationship between Jay and Maggie had been like. What began to emerge was a strange picture of the two. In her words at the time, "It's not a good relationship," and, "Maggie was less than thrilled about it." Moreover, Maggie had confided to her nearly lifelong friend that she was "a little scared of him [Jay]." Mary's own impression of Jay was that he was "very possessive" and had a "very jealous personality." He smothered Maggie. "He wanted every free minute of Maggie's time."

One incident stuck out in her mind that seemed to typify Jay's control issues. A few months before her death, Maggie and Jay had an argument that appeared to be on the verge of becoming violent. Maggie had walked Jay down to his car with the intent of breaking up with Jay. Margaret and Mary heard a loud "tearing" of footsteps down the hallway and stairs. Maggie ran into the apartment with Jay only a few steps behind her. As Maggie tried to close the door, Jay tried to push it open but the women inside were able to close and lock it.

Jay remained outside, banging to get in and yelling from the hallway to let him in. He barked, "You know I want to talk to you. Get out here!" Maggie screamed back, "No, I'm not coming out. Get out of here. I don't like you." Jay refused to leave, yelling to get in. Mary and Margaret got involved, fearing that he would break down the door, and told Jay to go away: "Maggie doesn't want to see you." Jay remained adamant, banging on the door until about a half hour later, when they threatened to call the police a few times. He finally left. But the breakup only lasted for a few days; Maggie was soon back with him.

Maggie confided to her friend about her relationship with Jay, saying to her on more than a few occasions that she wanted to break up with him but was afraid of him. Mary told her, "If you don't like him, break up." She kept saying that she was afraid of what he would do.

When police went back to discuss the incident with Margaret several weeks later, she remembered being threatened enough that she had taken out a rolling pin to defend herself if Jay were to get into the apartment. In going over their interviews with neighbors, Michael Griffin in apartment no. 17 remembered the incident well. He had told officers that the walls were so thin in the apartment complex that he often heard Maggie fighting with Jay, and on the occasion in question, he had opened his door and had seen Jay pounding on the door and yelling. He had finally called out to Jay himself, telling him that he was trying to get some sleep and to stop making noise.

Mary told officers that Maggie had confided in her that she still cared about Jim Downey. She even told Mary that she had had sex with Jim after his engagement, although Mary conceded that "Maggie would sometimes say things that weren't true." Seemingly contrary to this was information that Maggie's friend Lynn Van Geison provided. She said that while she believed that Maggie loved Jim Downey and had deep feelings for him, she was "staying away from him" since he was now engaged.

Lynn Van Geison had been friends with Maggie and had spent considerable time with Jay and Maggie socially. Jay had confided in her that the two of them were inseparable and really in love. Her own experience was that they were in a love-hate relationship and fought often. Lynn told investigators that Maggie may have been in such a tumultuous relationship with Jay because she may have felt that she couldn't have anyone else or did so out of fear that no one else would love her.

Ms. Van Geison confided to officers that Maggie had tried to break up with Jay before, but it never lasted more than a few days. Maggie would comment something along the lines of, "Nobody else stepped up to the plate." So she would drift back into Jay's arms again.

Their fights were not something that Maggie's circle of friends ignored. She told Lynn, "We fight all of the time, but, you know, he's always there." Maggie confided to Lynn that she was scared of Jay and what he would do if she broke up with him. She had gone so far as to say that Jay might become violent or "even kill her." On one occasion, they were at a Battle Creek bar called the Rafters, and Jay and Maggie once more became embroiled in another heated fight. Maggie and Lynn went into the women's restroom and Lynn asked why didn't she just break up with him? Maggie replied, "I've told you already, you know why I can't do that. I'm really scared of what he'd do."

Lynn hosted a dinner party at her house one night with a handful of couples, including Jay and Maggie. Once more, the two of them got into a fight. Jay stormed out of the house, apparently infuriated, running out to the car, hitting the car and then speeding off while Maggie was yelling at him, followed by some name-calling. Jay returned ten to fifteen minutes later, they made up, and he apologized to everyone. The dinner went on as planned.

These were not just recent occurrences. Jay and Maggie had been in a string of arguments starting when she was still living at home. The two of them got into an argument, and Jay persisted in calling the house, but Maggie refused to talk to him, so he would hang up. It was Lynn's belief that Maggie may have been trying to break up with Jay at the time. Maggie and the rest of the Humes went to bed, only to be awakened at 3:00 a.m. by Jay, standing outside knocking and calling, "Maggie, you open this door. I want to talk to you right now." According to Lynn, Mr. Hume got up and got really angry. Maggie went down and talked to him because she was afraid her father was going to hurt Jay. ("Mr. Hume protects his little girl," she added.) Jay and Maggie started yelling at each other, and Jay walked into the house, yelled at her some more and walked out the back door. He was so angry and frustrated that he broke the gate because he slammed it so hard when he departed. Despite Maggie's claims that she wouldn't get back together with Jay after that incident, a week later they were a couple again.

Police carefully probed at Maggie's sexual relations with her boyfriend/fiancé. Maggie told Mary that she didn't enjoy their sexual relationship at all—she found it boring and very quick, "nothing special." She didn't want to have sex often, and Jay would press her until finally she would give in to "get it over with." Maggie told her roommate, Margaret, that

Jay had pressed her for oral sex, but she refused to go along with it. For the investigators, these accounts from Margaret and Mary seemed to fly in the face of the image that Jay painted of the last time he saw Maggie. She had enticed him to have sex in his version of events and had done so in the living room of the apartment.

On November 5, 1982, at 2:32 a.m., two friends of Jay's were in a serious car accident on M-66—one was critically injured and the other was killed. At the time, the accident seemed tragic but routine—another case of kids driving drunk. Little did anyone realize the event's potential implications with the murder of Maggie Hume and how this horrible accident would drive much of the investigation almost two decades later.

A few days before Christmas, on December 19, 1982, Jay once more met with Detective Zuiderveen at the Battle Creek Police Department for an interview. The purpose of this interview was to confront Jay with the story presented by Sheila Guerra regarding the choking incident at the St. Phil volleyball game. Jay was adamant that he had never assaulted Maggie at St. Phil. He went so far as to claim that he had not attended a volleyball game that year at St. Phil at all. The officers had already spoken with Maggie's brother, John, who remembered seeing Jay attending several volleyball games with Maggie. When Detective Zuiderveen asked him about his statement during his polygraph, that he had been looking for her shoes in the closet prior to the discovery of Maggie's body, Jay claimed that he never made any such statement. He denied any involvement with the incident or Maggie's murder and walked out of the interview after two hours.

To many people, it might seem that there was ample circumstantial evidence to bring Jay Carter to trial. In this case, however, her father's local celebrity and position in the community worked against the family. Investigators and prosecutors took the investigation personally. Many felt that they couldn't afford to go to trial unless the case was airtight out of fear of failing Mike Hume and his family.

However, at the same time, the crime seemed simple to seasoned veterans like Detective Alan Tolf. "This is basically a boyfriend/girlfriend murder—plain and simple. Usually the first person you want to pull in is the last person that sees the victim."

As the holidays arrived in the winter of 1982, the investigation was still unfolding, still entertaining new tips and leads, but the case was no closer to being closed than the day of the crime.

ENTROPY

I used to dream it could last forever
But pipe dreams never come true
I'd be foolin' myself if I never
Thought something like this
Couldn't happen to you.
—"Man on Your Mind," Little River Band

The year 1983 crept in, and the officers working the Hume case still saw Virgil Jay Carter as the prime suspect. On January 3, Mrs. Hume met with the officers to tell them how Jay had seemed to know exactly where Maggie's diamond ring was during their visit to the apartment. She expressed to them once more that Jay seemed to know details about the crime that no one else knew about at the time.

The officers had also gone to St. Philip to attempt to validate Jay's story of going to the school the day Maggie was found and not being able to locate Mr. Hume. Interviewing the school staff, no one remembered seeing Jay come in and ask about where Mr. Hume was that morning. The school was not in session, and the close-knit community in the school remembered that horrible day quite vividly—just not Jay.

A few days later, officers executed a warrant on Jay to obtain his fingerprints. Only a few fingerprints were obtained at the crime scene, and since Jay admitted to being in the apartment the night of the murder, his fingerprints being found there would not have been a surprise at all. It is likely that the officers were asking for these at this time to keep up the pressure on Jay and make him think that they may have some evidence.

While he was providing the fingerprints, Detective Zuiderveen used the opportunity to once more ask Jay some questions about his previous accounts. Jay maintained that before he had gone to the apartment with John Hume, he had been to St. Philip to seek out Mr. Hume and had asked either a janitor or a secretary where he was. He had no explanation as to why people didn't remember him being there.

Jay told Detective Zuiderveen that his mother in Indiana had gotten a phone call from a person who said that "he was coming to see her and that he was going to kill her," allegedly as a result of Jay's being investigated in the death of his girlfriend. Jay's latest love interest, Julie Texter, had also received obscene phone calls. Zuiderveen suggested in both cases that if the women in his life felt threatened, they should reach out to their local police. Zuiderveen spoke with Jay's mother, who asked, "Do you think Jay killed Maggie?" It struck her as odd that a mother would even pose such a question about their child.

In February 1983, the case seemed to falter. Tips trickled in, but they were few and far between. The investigators had done all that they could at the time. With each passing day, Maggie's murder drifted away from the collective consciousness of the Battle Creek community at large. The Humes, however, were not going to let go of the case, and neither would Maggie's close friends.

Officers followed up on a tip provided by Linda Albrecht earlier in the investigation. She had conveyed to them that Maggie had once told her about a confrontation that had taken place at Kellogg Community College in the autumn of 1981. She had said that Billy Johnson had threatened Maggie either at home or the school.

In late January 1983, officers tracked down William Johnson, the man who allegedly had threatened Maggie months before her death. Johnson had met Maggie while he had been coaching volleyball at KCC—ironically the same volleyball team that counted Jay as a member. Johnson was a married man, but he had caught wind that Maggie was spreading rumors about him spending the night on Rose Street, presumably with another woman.

Angered, Johnson went over to the office on campus where Maggie had been working as a secretary in the sports offices and confronted her. He told her to watch what she told people. Apparently, it was done in such a manner that even by his own account, Maggie got upset and started crying as a result of the confrontation. After that incident, Johnson said that he had nothing to do with Maggie. He had seen her in the summer of 1982 with a group of people, and she had not displayed any reaction to his presence, so he assumed that the matter had been put to rest.

Still, from the officer's perspective, the fact that he had threatened Maggie was enough for them to probe further. Johnson claimed that he had no knowledge of where Maggie lived and that once the incident had occurred, it was done and over with as far as he was concerned. The officers contacted his wife, and she was able to confirm that William Johnson had been at home the night of the murder.

The next break came on April 20, 1983. Robert Smith, the manager of the River Apartments, and his maintenance assistant, Sandra Druskat, were cleaning out an area of junk near the maintenance building for the complex, only a few dozen yards from Maggie and Margaret's building. The area is about ten to fifteen feet square and surrounded by a wooded area on all but the north side. It is about twenty feet east of Stringham Road and forty feet south of the apartment driveway. The maintenance people for the complex used the area to regularly dump grass clippings, and some of the residents of the complex had tossed in the occasional bag of garbage. They had brought in a Dipsy Dumpster at about 2:00 p.m. to remove the debris from the area. While moving a pile of grass clippings, Sandra had found a brown wallet in the middle of it after hitting it with her shovel. Smith had checked it, and there were several photographs inside. They set it aside and completed their work, and at the end of the day, Smith took the wallet in to his wife, Mavis, to see if they could dry out the contents and discover who owned it. The clasp was already open. When he found the name "Hume" in the wallet, he remembered reading about Coach Mike Hume in the *Battle Creek Shopper* newspaper, so he looked up his phone number and called him. Mike contacted the police, who showed up and recovered the wallet.

There was no money in the wallet, but it was quickly identified as Maggie's. Officers interviewed both Smith and his former lawn maintenance man, Thomas Strong, to try and determine how the wallet had gotten there. Strong had worked for Mr. and Mrs. Barton, who were the managers when he had been employed at the apartment complex. He informed officers that he had never seen or touched the wallet and had not gone over a billfold while mowing the lawn. If he had, he told them, it would have been shredded. Strong didn't know of any residents dumping grass or garbage where the billfold was found. Strong said that he had never been in the apartment doing any work until the homicide victim's roommate, Margaret, had moved out.

THE MURDER OF MAGGIE HUME

This area was where grass clippings and some garbage was dumped near the apartment, as well as where Maggie's wallet was discovered. As you look in the distance, this area is the position from which future suspect Michael Ronning claims he saw Maggie through her window. *Provided via FOIA, Battle Creek Police Department.*

Thomas Strong was a bit of a hard-luck case at the time. He had been fired by the new manager of the apartment complex and had gotten a job at Godfather Pizza in Battle Creek, but he only worked there for three weeks, after which he was not able to keep up on his rent. He had bounced around from friends to his parents and so on, working a string of low-wage jobs to try to get by. According to Robert Smith, his former manager at the apartment complex, Strong was not a good worker and had "quite an attitude." A former employer described him as "cocky" and "always parading around—showing off."

The police department received a tip regarding Strong from a tenant in the apartment complex—that he had been seen peeking in the windows of some of the apartments. More intriguing was the fact that he had a set of master keys and was known to keep a watchful eye on the women who lived in the complex. The master keys included a key that worked on the balcony doors as well.

Jan Bell, who lived at the River Apartments, had been an acquaintance of Tom Strong's and confided with officers some time later about the somewhat shady goings-on at the complex. She had suspected that someone was getting into her apartment while she was away. She had taken the precaution of putting paperclips on top of her apartment door. Anyone coming in would unknowingly knock the paperclip down, telling her of the intrusion. She didn't suspect Strong of the action, but rather the building manager, Robert Smith. In one discussion that she had with Strong, Tom had told her that he had witnessed Smith outside her door, apparently listening in. Other than fallen paperclips, though, she could not identify anything that had been taken or disturbed.

When officers interviewed Thomas Strong, he talked about attending a toga party the night of the murder. Strong claimed that he did not know Maggie at all and had nothing to do with the crime. The officers suggested that he take a polygraph test and provide blood and hair samples; which he agreed to do. The results proved to be inconclusive because he appeared to be deliberately breathing hard and moving in the chair. Since the polygraph detects physical responses when questions are asked, Strong's squirming made his results invalid. Investigators still had a list of potential candidates who could validate Strong's story, but for the time being, they shelved pursuing him.

The focus never wavered far from Jay Carter. Given his performance in his first failed polygraph, the officers suggested that Jay come back in to take another examination. Jay initially agreed to come in and provide the polygraph test on July 6, 1983, but he never showed. When officers reached out to him to determine why had hadn't come in, Jay simply refused to take another test.

He wasn't alone in refusing additional polygraphs. Tom Carpenter, who had been very cooperative with the officers in the days after Maggie's demise, declined to come in as well. Carpenter said that he didn't see the point in coming in for a test since he had been nothing but cooperative. The officers were hard-pressed to disagree with him, as Carpenter had been forthright from the beginning of their investigation.

After Jay's refusal to come back in for a polygraph, the officers went back to his story once more, looking for any potential flaws. Jay had mentioned in numerous interviews that Maggie had complained of her car smelling of oil the night she had been killed. He had even gone so far as to talk about looking for the source of the aroma both at the nearby Ritzee and at Maggie's apartment. Since the murder, however, no one had detected the smell of oil.

Officers went to Trumble's Service Station, where Maggie and other members of the Hume family took their cars. They met with the manager,

Roy Kline, who knew Maggie both by name and on sight, as the Humes had been customers of his for years. She had purchased her AMC Hornet in 1982. Shortly after she had purchased it, she had brought the car in for an oil issue. Kline had replaced the valve cover gaskets on June 25, according to his records. Maggie had stopped by the station to purchase gas on the day that she had died; he remembered the event. Kline was sure that if she was having any sort of problem, she would have raised it with him at that time. She didn't.

AS THE SUMMER WANED and the one-year anniversary of Maggie's death approached, it became clear that a fresh perspective might help propel the case forward. Detectives Tolf and Mullen took over the lead on the case. Tolf brought with him experience on the investigation from day one, whereas Mullen had only recently been working it.

One of the plans that they devised was to open up with the Hume family about the suspicions they had regarding Jay. Usually in police investigations, the officers withhold information from even the victim's family for fear that it might leak and compromise the investigatory process. At this point, though, with a year going by, they hoped that the Humes themselves might be able to shed some insights about Jay that could help them.

The meeting with the Humes took place on August 16, 1983, the day before the one-year anniversary of Maggie's death. Detective Mullen was accompanied by Lieutenant Michael DeBoer. The officers laid out for the Humes the discrepancies in the various accounts that Jay had provided them. The Humes were asked to document their encounters with Jay, highlighting any information that seemed odd or out of place.

The results only seemed to confirm what officers suspected. Mike Hume's recollections of what Jay had said during those painful days around her funeral were chilling. Jay had stated to him that "whoever killed Maggie must have loved her." Jay also said that in his opinion, "It [her rape and murder] was an accident." Jay had confided in Mr. Hume's presence that Maggie was so neatly wrapped and her head was turned in such a way that it had to have been done with care.

Mrs. Hume's letter recounted Jay's discussion with Maggie's friends on the curb and comments he had made to her. Jay had claimed that he "knew it was an accident" and that he "knew they cared about her cuz they wrapped and covered her so neatly and carefully with a Snuggle-Sack." Jay also had stated several times that he knew that Maggie had been raped, yet the autopsy report was not compiled until two months later. In Mrs. Hume's

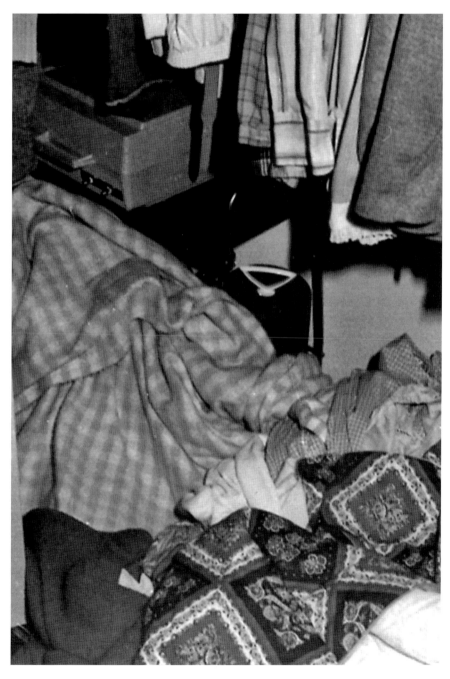

A more detailed image of the Snuggle Sack and blanket used to conceal Maggie's body. *Provided via FOIA, Battle Creek Police Department.*

letter, she noted, "Thought it strange to tell him something that we didn't really know to be sure about ourselves."

Jay had told Mrs. Hume that he knew that Maggie had been strangled—this again before the information had appeared in the Battle Creek newspapers. Jay related to her that he knew that her flight bag and wallet were missing. Officers knew that Maggie's purse had been found with her body and had not been discovered at the time Jay had been in the apartment.

Jay had also told Mrs. Hume that he "knew she was in a nightgown ready for bed." In fairness, when Jay had left, she had been in a nightgown, so that fact alone was not a stretch. It was when it was taken in the context of the other comments that it appeared more sinister. His final point was perhaps the most revealing. Jay "said it [the killer] was someone that knew her."

There were other little details that Jay had offered Mrs. Hume that differed from his account. He told her that he went to Maggie's apartment the night of the murder, and when he didn't find her there, he started back to his place and then turned around to come back to the Ritzee. Mrs. Hume couldn't have known about the flaws in Jay's timeline already. If he had driven toward his own apartment and then turned around, it would have given him even less time to accomplish all of the tasks he had detailed with the investigators.

Jay had asked Mrs. Hume during the period leading up to the funeral if Maggie was seeing anyone. It was a strange question to ask the mother of your murdered girlfriend, strange enough that Mrs. Hume noted it in her seven-page letter to officers: "Ask me if she was seeing someone else? Said no way. Not time to. Wouldn't anyway. Well, he guessed he thought that too."

In describing the blanket that he gave Maggie that night because she was cold, he told her it was lavender and then changed it to pink. In his words describing it, he said "he covered her up." In Mrs. Hume's comments, it was "a strange choice of words." Mrs. Hume was suspicious of this part of the story for different reasons. The apartment was air conditioned, and the two girls were tight on money. Maggie would have changed the thermostat rather than let the air conditioner continue running and burning electricity. Maggie's budget was so tight that she often went to the Hume house to eat lunch to save money.

Mrs. Hume prepared a list of anyone who might even remotely be considered as suspects in Maggie's death. Jay's name was first on that list. The others were all friends of Maggie's or individuals like Tom Carpenter, whom the police had already cleared through numerous interviews.

Detectives Mullen and Tolf went back to interview some of the key witnesses again. In a discussion the next day with Margaret, she remembered an incident where Jay and Maggie had been fighting in June the year before. Jay had angrily issued a command: "You don't date anybody!" Did Jay suspect that Maggie was seeing someone else? He certainly conveyed that concern with Mrs. Hume. Was his suspicion a potential motive for murder?

But once more, starting in the fall of 1983, the case seemed to enter a quiet period. Every tip was checked but proved less than helpful. Investigators in this period were concentrating on the automobile accident that involved Jay in November 1982 and the potential links to the case.

Dennis Mullen turned his attention away from Jay to try to follow other evidence and testimony. It was a time-tested police technique. His first pursuit was Thomas Strong, the young maintenance man who had deliberately compromised his polygraph test. Strong had indicated that he had been with a friend the night of the murder, William Barton. Strong had been living in the same apartment as Barton and his parents at the time of the murder. The senior Mr. Barton seemed to remember the party in question in Charlotte, Michigan, the night of the killing. According to his memory, the boys had come in after midnight, after he and his wife had gone to bed. He remembered the party because his son had been dating a girl in Charlotte who had been at the party, and when the two young men came home, they brought with them a red or orange pylon that they had found on the trip home. When Mr. Barton got up the next day, the cone was in the middle of the apartment's living room.

Detective Mullen had tracked down one of the party attendees, John Buckles, who had hosted the gathering. Buckles was a student at Central Michigan University, and his memory was different than that of Strong's. He recalled two parties at his parents' house, but he seemed to believe that they were in 1983 or 1980–81. His sister might have a better memory, but when her parents contacted her, to no surprise, she told her parents that she didn't remember any parties. Mrs. Buckles found their calendar for 1982 and found a reference to "Choir" and a dental appointment on the day in question. In other words, they were in town, and Strong's alibi for being at a party seemed to disappear. Then William Barton produced another party attendee, Kurt Sorensen, who remembered attending the party in 1982. A few days later, Mrs. Buckles contacted the police and indicated that she was indeed out of town in the period of Maggie's murder.

Attempting to corroborate Thomas Strong's story was an investigation all on its own. William Barton blew off at least four interviews with Detectives

Mullen and DeBoer. On October 9, 1984, the officers went to his apartment in Charlotte and asked him on the spot to come down for an interview, which he agreed to.

When the officers told him that John Buckles was unsure that the party was the night that Maggie had been murdered, Barton didn't flinch. He did remember that at the party, his girlfriend (now wife) had gotten gum in her hair, and the other partygoers had convinced her to use peanut butter to get it out. Barton said he was fairly certain that on August 17, they had picked up the orange road cone, although it could have been the night of the party.

The detectives asked Barton if he knew that Strong had failed his polygraph test, and Barton replied that he didn't know that. According to Barton, Strong had lost his job because he had been accused of stealing a revolver from one of the apartments. Strong also had a reputation for peeking in the windows of apartments and entering them without permission.

While Thomas Strong was a tempting potential suspect, there was little that could tie him to the case. He had no reason to rape and kill Maggie. There wasn't a shred of evidence that tied him to the crime. He had a set of master keys and would not have had to climb up on the balcony to gain access to the apartment. In fact, his constant presence at the apartment and his own testimony indicated that he knew Maggie had a roommate and had no way of knowing that she was or wasn't home that night, which pointed away from him as a viable suspect. By August 1985, Thomas Strong was refusing any further meetings with police and also refusing to take a follow-up polygraph test.

Mrs. Hume never faltered in her search for any hint or clue that might bring closure to her family. She contacted Detective DeBoer in September 1984 when she remembered that Maggie had told her that she had come home one day and found the sister of her roommate having sex in her bed. In fact, there had been an unidentified semen stain on the ruffled edging of the bed that had been in police custody for some time. Was this from the night of the attack or another incident? Officers had been able to confirm what Mrs. Hume had said with Mary. Maggie had indicated to her that Emily Van Winkle and her boyfriend had intercourse in Maggie's bed.

Detective Mullen contacted Margaret, who denied it outright. She knew of one instance where Cindy Brown and her boyfriend had used the phone in Maggie's room for forty-five minutes once—perhaps this was the instance to which Maggie had referred?

Emily Van Winkle was contacted at the University of Michigan. Emily's version of events contradicted her sister's. According to Emily, Margaret had allowed Emily and her boyfriend, Ronald Hutcheson, to use Maggie's room for a sexual tryst. Maggie had walked in on them, and the incident had been quite embarrassing.

Hutcheson was contacted and recalled the incident. He described Maggie's bedroom as having some stuffed animals in it and a dust ruffle. Margaret had let them into the apartment for the purpose of letting them have intercourse. Hutcheson volunteered samples of his blood and saliva to investigators.

Tests of the blood and hair samples had thus far proved inconclusive in the case. Maggie had Type A blood, Jay was Type B and Jim Downey was Type O. The stain on the dust ruffle from the bed was also Type O. In these years before DNA testing was widely used, the samples could only be compared against blood type. In this case, Hutcheson also came back as Type O. That did not mean that the semen stain was his or Jim Downey's—merely that it matched according to blood type. Likewise, there was no way to date the sample. Given that it was on a part of the bed that covered the box springs, it was not likely subject to regular laundry. In other words, the stain could have been there for months and may have had no connection whatsoever to the crime. For the investigators, it proved to be another dead end and, at worst, was an embarrassing incident for all parties involved.

In July 1985, Detective Mullen received a tip from Mrs. Hume that Maggie's cousin, Nancy, may have some information of use to him. Nancy Hume had spent several days at Maggie's apartment one month prior to her demise. Maggie had confided to her at that time that she was considering breaking up with Jay but was nervous about it.

Maggie had confided to Nancy that she still had feelings for her former boyfriend James Downey. According to Nancy, Maggie had opened up that Downey had a girlfriend and was engaged and that she (Maggie) didn't think they would ever get married, but she could see her and Downey dating.

When asked by Detective Mullen about her impressions of Jay, Nancy said that she knew him and somewhat liked him. He seemed possessive of Maggie, and the two of them fought "constantly." At Maggie's funeral, she noted that Jay didn't seem to show a lot of emotion over her death. She personally had never thought about Jay as a suspect until other members of the family began to talk to her.

The investigation continued its slide to "cold case" status. The reward level rose for information leading to an arrest in the case. A few days after the murder, the reward was $2,500. By September 1982, it had been raised to $3,000. An additional bump to $5,000 happened in 1984. By January

1985, the Silent Observer tip program was offering up to $15,000 for a tip that would lead to a conviction of Maggie's killer. Despite this large reward level, the number of tips diminished with each passing month.

A FLICKER OF HOPE came up on June 9, 1986, as a tip came in when a divorce attorney submitted to police the name of George Barrett Mackey of Kalamazoo. Mackey was divorced from his wife, and the attorney had represented her in the case. He suggested to authorities that they should look into him regarding Maggie's death.

On the surface, Mackey certainly looked like a possibility. In his divorce from his wife, he had gotten visitation rights to his child once every year. Each year, he took the child to California, where he resided. Mackey usually resisted returning the child from visitation, a constant legal issue for his ex-wife.

In 1982, Mackey and his ex-wife worked out a new visitation agreement, but he refused to sign it and instead left the state. In many respects, it proved to be a fortunate move for his ex-wife. Mackey remarried in California, and he and his new wife lived with her sister and several children. Three weeks into his marriage, one night, all of the members of the family had gone to bed except Mackey and his new bride, who were in the downstairs den watching television. In the morning, his wife's sister was discovered murdered, strangled by someone's bare hands. George Mackey was charged with the murder of his wife's sister.

The State of California granted him release on bond, and he came to Kalamazoo to pursue his visitation rights. Naturally his ex-wife refused, and Mackey sued to get custody of the child. While that case played out sitting on the court docket, Mackey left Michigan to return to California for his murder trial there. In Ogalla, Nebraska, he was arrested for running naked from a women's restroom at a roadside rest stop. The Nebraska authorities had him placed in custody on a "mental hold." After several days, the authorities in Lincoln, Nebraska, dropped the charges, and Mackey was released.

He eventually returned to Kalamazoo for a short time, still on bond, and then headed back to California. On the way, in Idaho, he was found standing on a riverbank with a hangman's noose around his neck and mumbling about his son being the second coming of Christ. He was arrested and detained for his own safety. According to the attorney who passed the tip to the Battle Creek Police, there was a missing four-year-old boy in a nearby town who had disappeared at the same time that Mackey arrived in Idaho. While no connection was ever proven, there was a clear implication that he was somehow potentially connected to that boy's disappearance.

Meanwhile, the murder charge for his second wife was dismissed by the court on a technicality. The prosecutors had failed to adhere to California's strict due process laws regarding a discovery order. Mackey's statements to the officers that he made when he had been arrested had been obtained, according to the court, "under questionable circumstances."

George Mackey clearly had mental stability issues, and looking at him as a potential suspect was something that could not be avoided. The biggest problem with him as a suspect was that he had no connection with Maggie Hume whatsoever. While he had lived in Kalamazoo, for all intents and purposes, it was thirty minutes and a whole other world away. If he did kill his second wife, he had strangled her, but beyond that, the circumstances were so dramatically different—to attempt to draw links to Maggie's death was a stretch at best.

In early 1986, one tantalizing tip came in secondhand from Mrs. Thiessen that seemed to point toward Jay Carter. She had been told by one of her daughters of a visit to Maggie's apartment prior to the murder. Her daughter said that while she was there, she had heard some noises coming from Maggie's balcony. Maggie told the girl, "Don't worry. It's only Jay. He does that all the time when I won't let him in." Margaret Van Winkle had also passed similar information to Detective Tolf. "Margaret told us that it was common for him to come in from the balcony. When he parked in back, he would climb up the balcony to get in. It wasn't out of the ordinary at all. Hell, I could have climbed up there."

This new information, while useful in establishing Jay's familiarity with climbing the balcony, was offset by the fact that Jim Downey had done it as well. Still, it was a pattern that was worthy of note. In the case against Jay Carter, it was merely another bit of circumstantial evidence. However, as circumstances would prove, reaching and stretching were becoming all that the investigators had to go on.

THE WRECK ON M-66

Driving faster
Driving past the scenery
On pretty view and
I feel as though I've
Got to control my
Reckless need to speed and speed.
— *"Speeding," the Go-Go's*

Just a few months after Maggie's death, Jay Carter was involved in a car accident (directly or indirectly) that resulted in a tragic death. As time passed, there seemed to be more links between this unfortunate accident and the death of Maggie Hume, although at the time those links were tenuous. Some of these connections would take decades for investigators to unravel.

On November 4, 1982, three months after Maggie's murder, a fatal car accident occurred in Battle Creek. It was a cold and windy night, typical for Western Michigan in November. Jay Carter, Kevin Danielson, Bartholomew "Bart" Chester Thiessen, Perry Lussier and Judy Rothwell all went to Nottke's Bowling Alley to celebrate their friend Terry "Tiny" Sheerer's twenty-first birthday. Turning twenty-one is a milestone in one's life—a time to celebrate and enjoy turning the legal drinking age. Ken Nottke's Bowling Alley was a popular hot spot for teenagers in Battle Creek. Bowling wasn't nearly as popular an attraction as the large arcade and pinball machine room that Nottke's had. In the era before Xbox and PlayStation, video games were more social, and Nottke's game center was a big draw for anyone over the age of sixteen. The video game room was dimly lit and reeked of spilled beer and a hint of cigarette smoke and sweat, but it was a hopping locale—something to do in a small town.

Jay, Terry and Kevin all worked at the Beer Company together. Terry worked with Jay processing the recycled bottles and cans, while Kevin ran the PC system and managed the routes for the company. Kevin was a 1980 graduate of Harper Creek High School and had been drawn into the small group through their jobs. Although they worked in separate buildings, Kevin had become friends with Terry because Terry had to call over and give Kevin the numbers from the recycling center. Terry and Kevin moved into an apartment and became roommates.

It was supposed to be a night of celebratory fun—good friends going out and drinking together. After a while, the group decided to drive to Rafters bar to continue the celebration. Rafters was a popular bar with music where the barely legal youth of Battle Creek gathered. It had a reputation for being dark and noisy, as well as a place where underage drinkers could mingle with those old enough to purchase them alcohol without much risk of being caught. Terry and Bart had been drinking heavily, mixing beer and whiskey throughout the night, while Jay had just a few drinks throughout the night. Terry and Bart were both described as "pretty loaded" when the group left Rafters at 2:00 a.m.

Kevin offered to take his roommate Terry home. Jay was adamant that Terry ride with him. Kevin argued back to Jay, saying that Terry was drunk, and he would rather just take him back to the apartment. Jay replied, "Nope, nope, nope." Kevin's thinking was that Jay didn't want to be stuck with Bart at the time—as he was better friends with Terry. Everyone planned and agreed to meet at Denny's for breakfast while walking to their cars in the parking lot.

Kevin and Judy headed to Denny's to wait for the rest of the group. From several witnesses' descriptions, Bart was so intoxicated at this point that both Jay and Terry had to physically put him in the back seat of Jay's car. One witness said he had been "poured" into the back seat of the car, in no condition to operate an automobile—or anything else, for that matter. Perry Lussier, a co-worker of both Jay and Terry at the Battle Creek Beer Company, witnessed Terry and Bart leaving the parking lot and saw that Terry got into the driver's seat. Perry noticed that Terry was also intoxicated, but not nearly as intoxicated as Bart, and that he was planning to take Bart to the Thiessen home on M-66 and return to eat breakfast at Denny's. Perry later told authorities that he doubted that Bart could even stand up, let alone drive a car on that cold November night.

The trio took Jay's car back to Nottke's Bowling Alley, with Jay being the driver, Terry in the passenger seat and Bart passed out in the backseat. Terry and Jay talked the entire way to Nottke's, and Jay claimed that Bart was asleep in the back seat the whole ride. At this point, the story varies—having either taken place at Nottke's or at Stanton's Grocery Store at B Drive and Capital Street. Jay later stated to the investigating police that he could not see who was actually driving Bart's car as it sped off Eastbound on Columbia then onto M-66. This testimony, coupled with the account provided by Terry, pointed to Bart as the driver of the car that fatal night. This became the "official" stance on who was driving—something that would be called into question in later investigations and would prove to have an important possible link to the Hume case because of Jay's involvement.

There were differing perspectives, however, to Jay's and Terry's accounts. It was the opinion of Kevin Danielson that Terry Sheerer was the driver.

Regardless of who was inevitably behind the wheel, Terry rejected Jay's offer to drive them back to Bart's house and entered the driver's seat. Jay pulled out and followed behind Bart's car but could not keep up with the speeding car. Jay was driving his 1980 red Ford Fiesta, a vehicle rarely referenced as a speedy vehicle. According to the initial police reports, Jay's account was that he lost sight of the car on M-66 southbound as Bart and Terry roared down the road at a high rate of speed. M-66 is a four-lane road, split by a wide boulevard—essentially a long, straight, flat section of road that was popular for fast driving thanks to its lack of curves. According to his account to the police, Jay continued to drive on to the Thiessen home. Once he arrived, Jay noticed that Bart's car was not parked outside. Jay alleged that he believed that Bart and Terry were playing a joke or trying to ditch him. Jay then claimed that he drove back to his apartment, and after he didn't see Bart's car at the apartment, he drove to Denny's. In his account given to the authorities, Jay said that after scanning the parking lot of Denny's, he decided to head back to his apartment for the night since he could not locate Bart's car. For him, the night was over.

Just moments before, at about 2:45 a.m., the gray Ambassador driven by Terry and Bart was traveling south when the vehicle left the roadway and hit the right shoulder at a high rate of speed. Although the pavement was dry, the vehicle drove back across the center line, leaving a skid mark of fifty-three inches, and onto the left shoulder on the east side of the roadway. The car then struck a four-foot-high embankment, causing the vehicle to flip over both length- and width-wise four complete times before landing on its top. The occupants were thrown during the rolls. Terry was found twenty yards south of the vehicle. Bart's shattered body was found about fifty yards away. The police officers who responded to the scene distinctly smelled alcohol on both men. Next to the vehicle lay a still chilled bottle of Miller High Life.

Both victims were taken by Emmett Township ambulance to Community Hospital in Battle Creek. Dr. Thomas Meier pronounced Bart dead at 3:32 a.m. He had bruising and lacerations to his face and chest, especially on his right side. His ribs and clavicle were fractured from the force of the impact and being thrown from the vehicle. His spleen had ruptured, and his left kidney had been lacerated. In the end, however, hemorrhagic shock took his life. His injuries, according to the officer, were consistent with him hitting the steering wheel, which seemed to indicate that he may have been the driver. The autopsy later showed that Bart's blood alcohol level was 0.13 percent. Terry showed scrapes and bruises on his arms and hips as well as to his head.

Kevin had stayed the night at Judy's, oblivious to the events that had unfolded with his roommate and Bart. The next morning, Terry's mother called to ask him if he was okay. He was stunned—why wouldn't he be? She went on to say that Terry was in the hospital in the intensive-care unit and that Bart had died in a car accident. Kevin immediately called Jay to see if he had known about the car accident.

The version of the accident told by Jay and his involvement here were very different than what Jay would later tell authorities. Jay told Kevin that Terry was driving Bart's car on M-66 when he "floored it," and Jay lost sight of the car. Jay told Kevin that he had seen the accident on M-66, but because of his prior involvement with the police in the Hume murder case, he did not stop to help his obviously critically injured friends. Jay told Kevin that he went to a pay phone at a gas station and called the police before he went home for the night. He added that he believed that the police were following him all the time. Jay told Kevin that he didn't know Bart was dead and said, "I'm not getting involved."

Even this account that Jay provided was questionable. The police recorded two phone calls that reported the accident. Mary Jill Spieldenner noticed the accident as she was driving home from work. Spieldenner drove to the Holiday Inn and called in the accident from the front desk. She then drove back to the scene of the accident and provided first aid until the arrival of authorities. Wayne Parks was on his way home when he noticed the vehicle flipped over. After arriving home, he called the police and drove back to the scene to assist with first aid. Wayne noticed several vehicles driving past the scene without stopping. There is no reference to an anonymous call coming in about the wreck. Either the police didn't record it or Jay never made the call to help his injured friends.

Kevin immediately went to Community Hospital downtown Battle Creek to see Terry and check on his condition. Terry's parents and uncle, Arthur Carl Morrison, were all present in Terry's room. The family greeted Kevin in tears and hugged him. Kevin told the family that he had spoken to Jay earlier in the day about the accident, and Terry's family seemed surprised, not knowing that Jay was involved. Kevin started to explain that Jay had said Terry was driving the car, but Terry's uncle interrupted him.

"The next thing I know is that I'm *thrown* into an empty room and pushed into a chair by Terry's uncle," said Kevin. The older Morrison reminded Kevin that he was a police officer and that the information Kevin was telling the family could cause damage to Terry. "You are never to repeat this conversation. If Terry was driving that car, then Terry will get pinned for this. He'll go to jail for a long time. And you don't want that, do you?" Morrison went on to tell Kevin that the police believe that Bart was driving, as it was his car and both occupants were thrown out of the Ambassador. Morrison told Kevin that since new drinking laws were put in place, Terry could get in trouble for driving and to "let the investigation go the way its going and that Bart was the one driving." Kevin started to speak up, but Morrison told him that Terry was unconscious and probably wouldn't remember anything about the accident when he woke up. Intimidated by the former police officer and guard at a prison in Coldwater, Michigan, Kevin begrudgingly agreed and went along with the story that Morrison and the Sheerer family had crafted. As far as they were concerned, Bart had been driving, and Terry had been merely another tragic victim of the horrid accident. At the time, it seemed an innocent enough white lie.

Donna Thiessen, Bart's mother, caught wind that Jay had seen the accident on the side of the road and didn't stop to help. Bart's father, Chester Thiessen, decided to pay a visit to Jay at the Beer Company to talk to him about the accident and what he might have seen. Jay refused to talk to him and left. As he departed, Mr. Thiessen noticed that Jay's car had fresh damage but didn't investigate further.

Terry Sheerer's recovery from his head injury was long and difficult. After he was released from the hospital, he spent most of the time at his parents' house. Terry's mother continued to pay her son's rent and half of the bills even though he was living at home, something that Kevin greatly appreciated. Terry's parents claim that they never told Terry that he was the driver during the accident. His mother worried that if her son knew, it would put him into a deep depression, and she encouraged Kevin not to bring the unpleasant matter up. Kevin continued to push that Terry needed to know that he was the one driving that night. Terry's parents answered, "Bart's insurance company has a lot of money, and Terry deserves it." The argument regarding the accident was a contributing factor in Kevin moving out of the apartment he shared with Terry.

Several months later, Terry decided to file an insurance claim against Bart's insurance company for the ongoing cost of his injuries. Once Kevin heard that Terry was suing, he confronted him. Kevin voiced his concerns to Terry about the deception of who was truly driving the night of the accident. Terry told Kevin, "Insurance companies have a lot of money, and I'm entitled to it." He seemed quite comfortable with the knowledge that he had been driving that night, although he claimed understandable memory issues of the evening in question. Kevin told him that he wouldn't lie in court to defend Terry. He had gone along with Morrison's and Terry's story so far, but now it was entering a new stage—insurance fraud. The scope of the injustices and crimes was growing. The small white lie to protect a friend had morphed into a new criminal activity—one that Kevin was clearly uncomfortable contributing to.

Terry went on further, telling Kevin that he "had something on Jay and wasn't concerned that Jay knew that Terry had been driving the car the night of the accident." Kevin took this to mean something relating to the Maggie Hume homicide case. The implication was that Terry may have heard Jay tell him something incriminating about the case and perhaps his involvement. Terry said that he wasn't worried about Jay "cause he's never going to go against me; he's never gonna say what you are telling everybody. Jay's going to knock your story down and say that Bart was driving. Your whole story is going to be nothing, void and null."

Jay himself told Kevin that he would deny telling Kevin that Terry was driving the car and that he saw the accident. Jay told Kevin it would be his word against Kevin's. Although they saw each other frequently, Jay and Kevin hardly spoke to each other. Kevin's only real ties to Jay were with his former roommate, Terry, and those relations were about to become even more strained.

Kevin Danielson moved on from the Beer Company to work at the Regional Medical Center in Battle Creek. While there, Kevin confided in a co-worker, Theresa Turley, about the accident involving his friends. As it turned out, Theresa was friends with the Thiessen family. She decided to send a letter to Bart's parents and the Prosecutor's Office to inform them that

Terry was committing insurance fraud. The letter was sent on September 27, 1984, and locally postmarked, and a few days later, three police officers were waiting for Kevin to arrive to work—assuming from the postmark that he had been the individual who had sent the letter. They took Kevin to a conference room and questioned him regarding the letter. It read as follows:

Dear Mr. and Mrs. Bart Thiesson [sic], I am writing you in regards to the accident that your son Bart and Terry Sheerer were in. I have found out that Terry is trying to sue your son's insurance company for injuries done to him in the accident. I feel that I must let you know something that is very important and something that I'm sure will put you both at rest. Your son, Bart, was not driving the car that night. Terry Sheerer was. Terry had no choice but to drive because Bart had already passed out once that night in the back of Jay Carter's car. Terry was bringing Bart back to your house and Jay was following so that he could take Terry to his home. Jay stated that he could not even see the accident happen because Terry was going at such a fast rate. I felt that you should know this information because I know that if I were a parent in your position, I too would agonize over the fact I had lost a son and that he had been the one driving when he knew he shouldn't have been, while so intoxicated. If I received this letter I would feel, if just a little burden taken off my shoulders. I know the truth will not bring Bart back or justify the accident, but then I don't feel that Terry should benefit from it either, in the way that he is trying to sue Bart's insurance company. I also feel that Terry had gotten away with enough without feeling any remorse at all. May God bless all of you and guide you. Signed, Anonymous.

P.S. I am sorry to bring up such a painful memory to you out of the blue, I just felt you had a right to finally know the truth.

A few weeks after the letter incident, Mr. and Mrs. Thiessen paid a visit to Kevin at work. The Thiessens, who were visibly upset, told Kevin that one of their daughters was dating Terry. "How could we possibly sit across the Thanksgiving dinner table looking at him, knowing he is responsible for killing our son?" That daughter later married Terry Sheerer.

Years later, Karen Thiessen, one of Bart's sisters, recalled an incident a couple of weeks before Bart's death when Bart had come home late from a night of drinking. Bart told Karen that Jay had told him that he had planned to kill Maggie Hume because he believed she was seeing another man. This conversation took place several weeks *before* Maggie's murder. Bart also claimed that Maggie had been getting threatening or strange letters prior to her death. Bart claimed that he didn't know why Jay had confided in him. If true, it would point to premeditation on the part of Jay. Of course, with Bart dead, there was no way to confirm the conversation.

On March 18, 1986, word reached authorities that Terry Sheerer had information on Jay that he wanted to share with investigators. He mysteriously cancelled the scheduled meeting at the last minute, leaving officers wondering as to what information he may have been able to provide.

For the Thiessen family, this seemed to add a sinister element to the auto accident that had taken Bart from them. Some of the family members began to believe that Jay may not have been just an ambivalent eyewitness to the death of their beloved son. Combining this with the damage that Chester Thiessen had seen on Jay's car, a theory emerged. Was it possible that Jay may have played a more active role in the accident? Was this an effort to cover up confessions he may have made to Terry and Bart about his involvement in Maggie's death? Had Jay intentionally run Bart's car off the road knowing that both Terry and Bart knew of his role in her murder? While this theory has no physical evidence or supporting material, some family members believed this to be true. Battle Creek is a small city regardless, and Karen Thiessen saw Jay at a party in either '83 or '84 and mentioned Maggie. Jay got very quiet and left the party, not wanting to talk about Maggie.

At first blush, this horrible accident appeared to be unrelated to the Maggie Hume murder. It would not be until cold case investigators reopened the files that they began to understand its potential significance. The accident does draw attention to Jay's character. Whether he intentionally caused the accident is unclear, but he did admit to seeing the accident involving his two close friends on the side of the road. He claimed that he didn't stop to help or even see if his friends were alive because of his involvement with the murder. Instead, he allegedly called police from a gas station and went back to his apartment. Whether Jay confided in Terry or Bart is unknown. Terry has refused to comment.

THE CONVICT

Those soft and fuzzy sweaters
Too magical to touch
To see her in that negligee
Is really just too much.
My blood runs cold…

— *"Centerfold," J. Geils Band*

By 1986, the Maggie Hume murder case seemed to be at a standstill. With little physical evidence and dead-end leads, the case was turning cold. Dennis Mullen was convinced at the time that Jay Carter may not have been involved with the murder. While still officially the prime suspect, Mullen began to go over the case again in hopes of finding a new lead or tip. His search took him far from the Hume case, spinning into several other murders around the country. The investigation turned up one man in particular: Michael Ronning.

According to Mullen's memory, "I was at the Homespun Restaurant with Joe Newman when we bumped into Mark Crawford from Channel 41. He was a good reporter and had interviewed me several times. We started talking about some cases, and he mentioned the [Patricia] Rosansky case. He said, 'If I had been in the jury, I would have voted guilty because I hated Cress's lawyer more than I thought he was guilty.' Ted Hentchel was his attorney. I don't want to say anything bad about him…but he was the worst. One time, in court, his own client knocked him out of his chair. He was simply the worst. Crawford said that Cress was probably innocent, but the jury hated Hentchel so much that they convicted him."

That got Detective Mullen thinking about the case. While Thomas Cress was currently serving time for Patricia Rosansky's murder, there still was no physical evidence that pointed directly at him. There were several questionable people who testified against Cress; at least one perjured herself in her testimony—she admitted that she had lied. He began to share his concerns with his supervisor, Joe Newman.

Joe Newman had been promoted to detective in the Battle Creek Police Department in 1985 and was in command of the Major Crimes Unit (Homicide). He had attended St. Philip High School while Mike Hume had been the coach there, graduating in 1971. His affiliation with the school and Maggie's case was cemented from those days. Newman graduated from Michigan State University but had returned to his hometown to work in the community in which he had grown up. His personal motto was "Always do the right thing." Newman's own recollection of his initial involvement with the case was Dennis Mullen driving him around town, talking about crimes in the area and showing him where various bodies had been found. According to Newman, it was during this period that the two men began to draw correlations between some of the crimes.

Regardless of the sequence of events and the timing of when people claimed they began to draw potential links between various crimes, no one can deny that Michael Ronning became retroactively connected to the Hume case on September 19, 1986. A letter from Arkansas State Police arrived at the Battle Creek Police Department saying that the state police had arrested Michael "Mike" Ronning for the murder of Diana Henley in Jonesboro, Arkansas. Mike Ronning admitted to murder, as well as killing multiple times in multiple states, but provided no details. The state police discovered that Ronning had lived in Battle Creek on and off throughout his life and decided to contact the local police department to investigate any unsolved cases in the county.

Michael Ronning was raised in Battle Creek, Michigan, and was a man with a questionable past. As a young teenager, Ronning was known to drink, smoke marijuana and fight. There are some unconfirmed reports that say that Ronning liked to torture animals. Another police interview mentions him attacking a female family member with a hammer. A high school dropout at age seventeen, Ronning spent time serving in a state prison for burglary and stealing cars. After his release, he traveled the country, never staying in one area for more than a few months, often getting arrested for minor offenses. He was arrested in the late 1970s for attempted rape and armed robbery in California and indecent exposure in Oregon, and he was arrested on suspicion of raping a drugged prostitute in San Diego. He found work in construction and developed an addiction to drugs.

Ronning's brushes with the law escalated to murder in January 1986. Ronning started working for Darryl Meredith, a carpenter in Jonesboro, Arkansas. A few weeks later, Darryl had driven Ronning to his home in order to pay him his weekly salary, which he paid in cash. While stopping by at Darryl's home, Ronning was introduced to Darryl's nineteen-year-old girlfriend, Diana Henley. Ronning watched as Darryl reached into a coffee can for a roll of bills in order to pay him for his work.

On January 6, 1986, Darryl left for work, leaving Diana at his home alone as usual. Ronning didn't show up to the job site that morning. When Darryl returned from work for the day, Diana wasn't at the house. Her car was still parked in the driveway, and her coat was where she had left it. Her purse, cigarettes and empty billfold were left on the couch. Upon checking his coffee can, he noticed that $700 in cash was missing from the hidden can, and a Bowie knife was missing from the kitchen. Darryl contacted the police, who later came to interview him at his home. Once they established Diana as a missing person, the police talked to a few neighbors to see if anyone had noticed anything suspicious.

One neighbor reported seeing an old rusty white car parked in front of Darryl's driveway in the early morning hours after Darryl had left for work. Darryl recalled seeing Ronning driving a car of that description. Darryl also told police that Ronning would have known exactly where his hidden coffee can of cash was located since he had seen him retrieve money from the can just a few days before.

Diana's body was discovered by hunters seventeen days after she was reported missing. She was found with her hands and feet bound up, lying on the ground in her red bathrobe covered in branches about thirty miles from Darryl's house. The autopsy showed that she had been stabbed multiple times in the throat with a large knife. Due to the time lapse between her death and her body actually being found, it was unable to be determined if she had been sexually assaulted.

Police didn't waste any time tracking down Ronning for questioning. They went to his residence in Pocahontas, Arkansas, and he was found hiding in bushes about seventy-five feet behind his house. Once police spotted him, he started running into a deep wooded area. Police took off after Ronning, eventually tracking him down. Ronning denied any knowledge about the disappearance of Diana Henley. Ronning did not have any money on his person at the time of questioning. His wife, Vicki Ronning, reported that Mike had come home the day of the murder around noon, saying that he didn't have any work for the day. She also reported that he had several $100 bills with him at that time.

Multiple witnesses reported seeing Mike Ronning driving his white-colored car near the area where Diana was later found. Crime laboratory experts testified that fibers found in Mike's car floor mats matched those on the bathrobe Diana was wearing when her body was found. Ronning's wife, Vicki, provided police with the clothing Ronning had worn the day that Diana had disappeared. Red fibers from Diana's bathrobe were also found on his clothing. Mike Ronning was charged with Diana's murder, convicted and received life without the possibility of parole, narrowly escaping the death penalty.

This incident was not the first that made Michael Ronning look suspicious. Darryl later told police that he and Ronning had stopped at a convenience store one day for coffee. While in the store, a red-haired teenage girl entered. Mike got up from having coffee and deliberately followed the girl around inside the store. Mike pretended to look at a magazine, although he was really stalking the young girl. When she left the store, Mike followed her out to her car and returned inside a few minutes later with a partial license plate number written on a napkin. Darryl asked his employee what he was doing, and Mike told him he was planning to bring his wife, Vicki, to the area in a few weeks and drop her off to go shopping while he looked around for the girl's license plate. He said if he found her, he was going to get into her car and "get some" from her.

When Darryl mentioned that Mike's wife might get upset with him, Ronning replied that she wouldn't dare make any problems with him over that. He then went on to say that there was a time when he almost got caught fooling around. While he was living in an apartment complex in Michigan, he "got some" from a redheaded girl. The day after the incident, Mike heard a co-worker talking about how Mike had cheated on his wife. Ronning got angry and hit his co-worker with a 2x4 plank. He and Vicki had left Michigan for Texas after that incident.

While these incidents don't exactly pin Michael Ronning as a murderer, an eerie connection with the Maggie Hume case came to light. Ronning had been living in the same exact apartment complex in Battle Creek the night Maggie Hume had been murdered. In fact, the apartment he shared with his brother was directly underneath Maggie and Margaret's apartment.

Steve Ronning, Mike's brother, confirmed that Mike, Angie Henson and Vicki all lived in a ground-level apartment at River Apartments. Steve was paralyzed from the neck down due to a swimming accident he had in the military. Due to his condition, he required assistance with daily activities. Living on the ground floor was ideal for someone with a handicap. He invited Mike to live in the apartment with him, with the hopes that his brother would be of assistance to him. Documents at River Apartments show that Steve and Mike Ronning moved into the ground-level apartment about four days before Maggie and Margaret moved into their apartment. After coming to Battle Creek, Mike met Vicki, his future wife. Shortly after they started dating, Vicki also moved into the apartment with Steve and Mike. Vicki, as it turned out, is Mike's second cousin—both having common relatives in Arkansas.

Angie Henson also moved into the apartment to assist with Steve. Angie was under the impression that Mike and Vicki would teach her exactly how to take care of Steve and understand his daily routines.

On the night of Maggie's murder, a group of friends had gathered at Steve's apartment for a get-together. After a few hours of drinking with friends, Mike left the apartment at about 11:30 p.m., saying that he was going fishing. Vicki did not see or hear from Mike after he left the apartment. Angie stated that she had gone to bed at about 2:00 a.m. and that Mike had still not returned. She said he was at the apartment when she woke up early the next morning.

Police had come by the apartment late in the day on Wednesday to advise them that a murder had taken place in an apartment above them. When the police asked who all lived in the apartment, Angie did not list Mike or Vicki since they were planning to leave for Texas shortly. Mike returned to the apartment after the police had left. He approached Angie, grabbing her by the elbow and saying, "You didn't tell the police that I was out last night, did you?" Angie denied telling the police anything and felt scared of Mike from that incident.

The next day, Mike and Vicki Ronning left for Texas, as they had planned to do for several days, leaving Angie behind with few instructions on how to take care of Steve. They stayed with Steve Odette in the Dallas area after telling him that they "were on the run." Mike said he had ripped off a dope dealer for nearly $3,000 and that's why he had left Battle Creek so abruptly. Vicki Ronning would later recount to Detective Mullen how her husband would come home from work one day and announce that they were leaving for another city immediately. Vicki described the couple living in California, Texas, Michigan, Arkansas and Louisiana over the years.

Detective Mullen focused on the fact that Michael Ronning, a convicted murderer, lived under Maggie Hume's apartment and abruptly left the following day. It was a coincidence that would consume years of his life.

Vicki and Michael Ronning were cousins and shared a grandmother who lived in Arkansas. Detective Mullen reached out to the mutual grandmother for billing invoices in order to track Michael's whereabouts over the years. These invoices would later prove that Ronning was living in Battle Creek when Maggie was murdered, in Arkansas when Diana was murdered and in Texas and California when two other women were murdered. He was also in Michigan when Patricia Rosansky and a Bellevue girl, Carrie Evans, were slain. Detective Mullen started to talk to Ronning's other family members around the country and found some interesting links between Ronning's travels and unsolved homicide cases.

A cousin who lived in Arlington, Texas, brought up an instance involving his girlfriend's disappearance and death. In September 1982, just one month after Maggie Hume's murder, twenty-year-old Annette Melia left the cousin's home one evening to walk to a convenience store. Mike had been visiting his cousin at the time. Annette's body was discovered by squirrel hunters three years later in a dumping ground in Bedford, Texas. Her body was covered with roofing shingles. In 1991, sixteen-year-old Melissa Jackson's body was found covered with plywood just eight hundred yards from where Annette's body had been found. She had been missing from her home in Grand Prairie, Texas, since 1983. After a check of billing invoices, it was discovered that Mike Ronning was in the Grand Prairie area when she had disappeared.

On July 6, 1985, thirty-eight-year-old Sandra Williams was raped, bound and strangled with a telephone cord at the Berry Hotel in Sacramento, California. She was last seen checking into the hotel room with a white male. That summer, Ronning was living in Sacramento and working in hotels throughout the area, including a job he held at the Berry Hotel as a handyman. He had an access key to every room at the hotel as part of his job.

Was it a pure coincidence that Michael Ronning had been in each city where a young woman disappeared? Multiple murders, all throughout the early 1980s, took place when he was in the vicinity. Either Ronning had terrible timing with moving around the country, or, as Dennis Mullen began to believe, Michael Ronning was a traveling serial killer.

In late 1982, Mike and Vicki got married and moved back to Battle Creek, in the same apartment with Steve and Angie. They decided to have a New Years Eve party on the last day of 1982. Gerry Olsen, a partygoer, was given a ride home after the party by Mike, Vicki and an unidentified woman. In the conversation in the car, the Maggie Hume murder was brought up. In that context, Olsen asked Mike if he had lived in the apartment building when the murder occurred. The unknown woman spoke up at that time and said, "Yes, and the police would have arrested Mike for it if I hadn't lied and told them he was in Texas at the time." According to Olsen, Ronning just kind of grinned and looked around. He neither confirmed or denied her statement or made any comment at all. Detectives made attempts to locate and identify the unknown woman who made the statement but were unable to do so.

DETECTIVE MULLEN WAS ON shaky ground in terms of jurisdiction. While Maggie Hume had been killed in the Battle Creek city limits, Carrie Evans had died in Bellevue and Patricia Rosansky had been killed, presumably, in Bedford Township—putting two of the murders out of his jurisdiction. Mullen presumed that he had some rights to probe into the Rosansky case because of the recanting of one of the witnesses who had testified against Thomas Cress. "She did that in Battle Creek—in our court. That perjury took place in Battle Creek, and that was what gave me jurisdiction to look into the Rosansky case." At best, it was a reach. The Michigan State Police had managed the original case in the Rosansky case, and the Calhoun County Sheriff's Department had led the investigation in the Evans case.

Sometime between 1987 and 1989, Dennis Mullen met with then-prosecutor Conrad Sindt to discuss his ever-expanding theories regarding Michael Ronning. "Well, a discussion arose. He had...he had come to my office to discuss, I believe, the Hume investigation, and we were discussing that. He described a number of other cases which he thought that Ronning was a suspect, and in the course of that, amongst other cases—some of which were not necessarily in Calhoun County cases, as I recall—he expressed the belief or the thought, I believe he said, 'I think Ronning killed Patty Rosansky.'"

Sindt had prosecuted Thomas Cress for the Rosansky murder and took the news seriously. "Well, I asked him what he knew about the Rosansky investigation because I had not...I had been involved in that throughout and had never dealt with him in that case, and in fact, that wasn't a Battle Creek Police case. That was a State Police case, so I was surprised that he was rendering that belief or that thought, and I asked him what he knew about it and, specifically, had he read the reports or read the trial transcript or talked to the State Police. And he indicated to me he had not." The prosecutor even gave Mullen the name of the officer who handled the case. "I said to him there was going to have to be something developed here before I can look at this."

Detective Mullen did *not* make the two-and-a-half-mile trip to the Battle Creek State Police Post to review the case file associated with the Rosansky case. While he engaged with police departments in Texas, Florida, Arkansas and California, he did not look at the case file for Patricia Rosansky for years.

Conrad Sindt, for his part, did not pass on the information to the incoming prosecutor, Jon Sahli. Without actual evidence presented to him, all he had was Dennis Mullen's theory regarding Ronning's involvement.

DETECTIVE MULLEN FELT THAT the way to get information on Ronning was through his wife, Vicki. During an interview with Vicki in September 1987 while being incarcerated for a drinking and driving conviction in Calhoun County Jail, she mentioned to Mullen that she had bought Mike a certain pair of shoes from Sears prior to the Hume murder. She went on to say that Mike was wearing those shoes the night of Maggie's death. Vicki was provided with a 1982 Sears catalogue and identified the shoes she had gotten for Mike. Investigators contacted Sears and eventually the manufacturer of the shoe soles for the particular model shoe. Copies of the soles were obtained from the manufacturer. The soles matched the shoe print found on the utility box below Maggie's balcony with the grass clippings on it. Dennis Mullen didn't have the actual shoes, only Vicki's word on the shoes—a popular brand of deck shoes sold in the hundreds of thousands.

Dennis Mullen spent a great deal of time interviewing Vicki Ronning, doing everything he could to probe her with information that he knew from the Hume case, looking for links to potentially tie Michael to the crime.

At the time that the letter had come in from the Arkansas State Police tipping him off about Ronning, Detective Mullen carried at least six open homicide or sex offender cases involving children. With his digging into the Hume case, he had little to tie Maggie's death to Ronning other than a potential set of shoes and some remarkable coincidences...and his gut feeling. Detective Mullen packed his bags in 1991 and headed to Arkansas to try to talk to Michael Ronning about his possible involvement in a few open homicide cases in Calhoun County. Ronning refused to talk, only telling Detective Mullen to "piss up a rope."

Detective Mullen approached the new Calhoun County prosecutor, Jon Sahli, with his commander, Joe Newman. Newman and Mullen explained that they believed that Ronning was linked to "Maggie Hume and other murders" in Calhoun County. Sahli agreed that Ronning should be re-

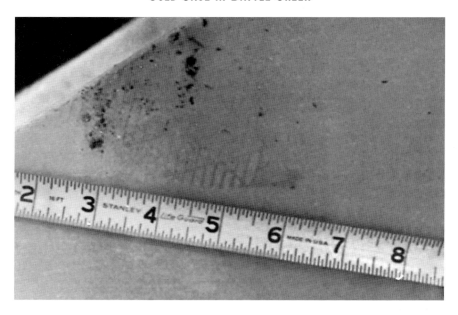

A footprint on the utility box leading up to Maggie's balcony. According to Dennis Mullen, this matches a brand of shoe that Michael Ronning owned in 1982. *Provided via FOIA, Battle Creek Police Department.*

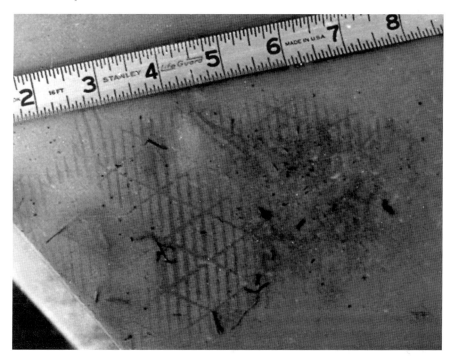

A distinct footprint, most likely of the killer, leading up to the balcony of the apartment. *Provided via FOIA, Battle Creek Police Department.*

interviewed. Although Mullen and Newman ardently believed that they had mentioned the Patricia Rosanksy murder as part of these discussions, Prosecutor Sahli's recollection and notes only mentioned the Hume case. The details of these discussions would have ramifications on Ronning's connections to Maggie Hume in the years to come.

Detective Mullen headed back to Arkansas on January 13, 1992, to meet with Ronning once again. This time, Ronning was willing to talk, but under conditions. According to Mullen, Ronning indicated that he was responsible for as many as six homicides and, according to Mullen years later, "could clear the man that was in prison for the Rosansky murder." Ronning offered to take a polygraph to prove his claims. But he would only cooperate once a deal was brokered to get him to a Michigan prison.

Keith Hall, an attorney-at-law in Arkansas since 1989, worked as a public defender and was asked by a circuit court judge in Arkansas if he would be interested in representing Ronning in brokering a deal to return him to Michigan. Keith Hall flew to Michigan on August 22, 1992, in order to meet with police officers and the Calhoun County Prosecutor's Office. Detective Dennis Mullen picked up Hall from the airport. While on the way to the Battle Creek Police Station, Mullen drove Hall to the location where the body of Patricia Rosansky had originally been discovered.

A meeting was held at a local bar restaurant, JW Barleycorns, with Calhoun County prosecuting attorney Jon Sahli, Chief of Detectives Joe Newman and Assistant Prosecuting Attorney Matthew Glaser. The purpose was to discuss Ronning's connections to murders in Battle Creek, specifically Maggie Hume. The general idea was to get Michael Ronning to Michigan, see if he would confess to any homicides and get the governor to agree to keep Ronning in Michigan. Jon Sahli stated that he did not give any facts or information regarding any of the open homicide cases to Hall because "I wanted something from the mouth of Mike Ronning that no one else could possibly know. Something that would convince me that he was, in fact, guilty of the murder of Maggie Hume." The approach should not have been foreign to the officers—Ronning was to be kept in the dark about the crimes. No one, not even Newman, knew at the time that information was already being passed inadvertently to Ronning's attorney in the form of showing him where Patricia Rosansky's body had been dumped.

Accounts of what happened after the meal differ. Sahli only recalled discussing the Hume case. Hall recalled discussing Ronning's possible involvement in the murders of Maggie Hume, Carrie Evans and Patricia Rosansky. Due to Ronning's lifestyle of moving from state to state at the drop of a hat, Mullen considered that he might have been involved in murders in other states.

After the discussion with Ronning's attorney, the group came to the consensus that without a confession by Ronning, there was little or no case against him. Hall later would testify in court that the group reached a tentative agreement that Hall would speak to Ronning about confessing to the murder of Maggie Hume and then plead guilty to first-degree murder. After the trial, Ronning would be transported to the Michigan Department of Corrections, where he would serve out a mandatory sentence of life in prison without the possibility of parole.

Keith Hall returned to Arkansas and spoke with Ronning regarding a possible confession. Ronning agreed to confess to the murder of Maggie Hume. In order to get Ronning transferred to Michigan, a deal had to be made with the governors' offices in each state. It was a complicated process at best.

A search warrant was issued against Ronning for hair, fingerprints and other searchable evidence. The affidavit that was issued to Ronning contained Maggie's name, birth date, details of the crime and investigation, how the body was recovered and its position in the closet. Maggie's physical appearance was also provided, along with her cause of death—listed as strangulation. When Dennis Mullen executed this search warrant, the affidavit that had been drawn up and handed to Ronning and his attorney had critical details about the crime—more than had ever been made public in newspaper accounts.

On October 13, 1992, Assistant Prosecutor Matthew Glaser sent a letter to Keith Hall explaining in detail what the Calhoun County Prosecutor's Office wanted to happen with the confession and transfer. The letter only mentioned the Maggie Hume case. Hall interpreted the letter to mean that Calhoun County was only interested in the Hume case. Hall eventually decided to take a position with a Prosecutor's Office in Arkansas and stopped representing Ronning.

Keith Hall testified in the Jackson County Circuit Court that Detective Dennis Mullen told him "everything about the two murders" (Hume and Rosansky) and that he was permitted to look through police files on the murders. The prosecutors were not present when the information was given to him, which seemed to fly in the face of Jon Sahli's orders that Ronning was not to have access to any information about the case. Hall's recollection was that at the time, he had no idea that one homicide already had a convicted murderer sitting in a jail cell (Thomas Cress); he was under the assumption that both murders mentioned were unsolved. Hall later stated in court that he took notes on the Patricia Rosansky and Maggie Hume murders since both cases had been identified during his meeting when the prosecutor was present. In later court testimony, Detective Mullen admitted that he did give Hall information concerning the homicide cases and that he had never been told by anyone not to release any facts. Even if he had not been told by Sahli about sharing the information, it should have been a red flag for him. Ronning had not yet confessed and providing him information would let him tailor his confession to the details that were provided.

The strategy that the Prosecutor's Office executed involved not giving Ronning everything in his deal. It prepared an offer and provided it to him, deliberately letting it sit. Several years later, in a court proceeding on the Rosansky case, Matthew Glaser recalled the strategy:

> *The idea was we made him his offer. It was just supposed to lay there. We knew he would reject it because he's not in control. I mean that's part of this psyche that he was supposed to have and nothing really was being done at this point. We were waiting for him to get sick of being in Arkansas and finally fess up, make the statement. And that—that you know, that was supposed to be all that was going on and then we had this melt down with Joe and Denney and it turned out that Denny had actually continued during this course of time to correspond with him and I don't know if negotiations would be the right term, but at least give the impression that we were continued to negotiate which was undermining the whole idea of why we made the offer that we made and just let it sit there.*

Detectives Newman and Mullen were frustrated with the little progress that had been made in making the deal happen. They met with the chief of police and State Representative Bill Martin to try to get help in getting movement on the matter by the Prosecutor's Office. To further the pressure, they contacted the local television station, Channel 41, and convinced it to run a four-part series on the Prosecutor's Office not moving fast enough on a confession in the Hume case. People expect the police and prosecutors to work together toward a common goal. While their motivation (resolving the Hume case) may have been noble, their actions were woefully misguided. The two officers were exceeding their authority on the matter by going to politicians and the press, deliberately causing a rift with the Prosecutor's Office that would last for years.

Cold Case in Battle Creek

It wasn't until late 1996 that Michael Ronning was brought to Battle Creek, Michigan. He agreed to confess to not one but three homicides. Ronning's confession was about to change the Hume case for years to come.

In return for confessing, Ronning would be offered a chance to serve out his life sentence in Michigan. By taking the deal, Ronning wouldn't be extradited on any other murder convictions to those states that had the death penalty, including for the Texas and Florida homicides to which he may have been linked. Accepting Michigan's offer was a perfect package for Ronning; he would be moved to a prison much closer to his family, who would most likely visit him. Arkansas governor Mike Huckabee and eventually Michigan governor Jennifer Granholm agreed to transfer Ronning to Michigan on the condition that he passed a polygraph and provided truthful accountings for his crimes. It was on this last point that police and prosecutors would be split. Was his confession indeed truthful?

In 1997, Ronning also took a polygraph test where he answered "yes" to the statement, "Is three the true number of people you killed in Michigan?" While he responded that was true, there was no way of knowing what three murders he intended to confess to until the day he did finally tell authorities.

Ronning's initial confession for the Maggie Hume case is as follows:

> *Alright, I don't remember any dates with the first incident that occurred in the state of Michigan. Um I think it was like 1982 or 1983 somewhere around in there. I was staying at my brother's apartment on Stringham Road. Uh, the girl is Maggie Hume, who I found out later through you and your investigators. Uh, I left my apartment maybe about 11:30 at night, 12:30 at night, something like that to go down to the corner to go fishing. I was coming down from cocaine, I had run out of cocaine. I was firing it up intravenously and uh, and things started getting weird coming down [garbled]. I walked around the apartment on Stringham Road and down Stringham Road of the corner of the curve there, where the river bends. When I was walking down there, I looked up and seen her in the window. Uh, I went down and uh threw my fishing pole in the water—to the bank in the water and uh went back, scaled the wall, got on her terrace…I guess that's what you call it…and I went through the window; to the left if I'm on the terrace facing the apartment I went to the left into that window. Uh, went into her bedroom, uh, immediately hit her and grabbed her around the throat and uh she…I guess out of fear uh, said it was okay to do anything—so I had sex with her. Uh, when that was over, I strangled her, uh, I realized what I did—even though I meant to do it—I realized the*

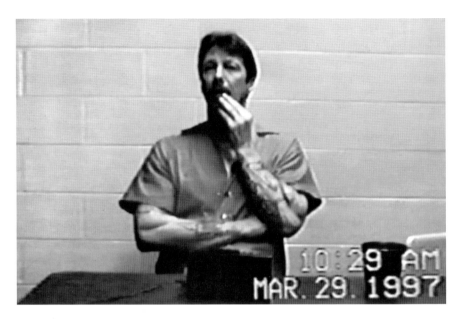

Michael Ronning during his confession. *Provided via FOIA, Battle Creek Police Department.*

enormity of the action I'd just done. And to throw the police off of uh…there should have been trauma to her neck, uh, I kicked her neck two or three times to try and hide the fact I strangled her. I threw her in the closet; covered her up with her own clothes…left…tried to make it look like a robbery, took her wallet. It was in her purse on her dresser. I took it to the end of the parking lot and buried it. And uh, and went back to my apartment. When I left her apartment, I left through the door of the apartment inside the apartments. I don't uh, remember if I went out on the parking lot side or the street side, but I went back down to where I had a fishing pole and stuff and brought it back up, come back up where I had the fishing pole uh, and I stopped up at the end of the parking lot there, around the curve side of Stringham Road and uh, buried her wallet. I don't know if there was any money in it or anything—I buried the whole thing. I came back to the house. Uh, went to sleep. I was able to. I got up the next morning, the cops were there, police were apparently investigating, so…we were already packed up to go, because we had already planned on going. So my wife and I, we left that day. We were going to leave the following day but we left that day. And that was it.

Later during follow-up questions to his confession, he revealed more: "I believe, but I'm not positive, but I believe the head was facing the inside of the closet. Uh, if I said I performed sex with her, it was uh, she basically consented out of fear I would imagine. Uh, my wife informed me at one time that there was anal sex involved. If that's true, it was inadvertent. I didn't know that I was doing that as far as anticipating that. Uh, I can't remember, anything else—I didn't bother anything else, I didn't bother anything else in the apartment. I went up there specifically to kill her, and I did—and I left."

Ronning was asked to describe what Maggie was strangled with. "My arm," he said as he made a gesture as if he were choking her with his arm/inner elbow. He was asked how he got up on the terrace:

> On a round meter thing, some type of meter-thing, that's how I got up there. I climbed up that. I'm pretty good at climbing. Uh, in my work, my line of work as a carpenter, I had to do a lot of climbing and uh, a lot of balancing and so-forth, so I can climb up what most people find pretty difficult. You mentioned a terrace. That's where I went up the wall and got on the terrace. I went to the left. It was either inside the terrace or on the right outside of the terrace. There was a door and a window, and I looked inside that window. The window had a screen on it. Uh, I was careful that I didn't leave any fingerprints. The window was open. Uh, I popped

The maintenance shed, near where the wallet was discovered. Past this area several hundred feet is also the area from which Michael Ronning claims he saw Maggie through her window. *Provided via FOIA, Battle Creek Police Department.*

the screen off—I think there was a screen there, I popped the screen off [garbled] *I can't tell, I thought I did, I couldn't tell* [garbled]. *When I left, I left through the apartment so it should have been unlocked. Of course if somebody else was there and located the body before you guys did,* [garbled] *but the apartment should have been unlocked.*

When asked to describe Maggie's wallet:

Her wallet was in her purse. It was leather purse with her wallet. What'd it look like? Uh, I don't really have much of an idea...I can tell you exactly where it was at though. It was at the uh, you know where that West Michigan and Stringham Road is? It's at the West Michigan end, at the other end, where Stringham Road turns around at the end of the parking lot and maybe ten feet, out into the—there's got some little trees—maybe ten feet out of there where they got a bunch of leaves looked like they'd been raking up leaves up in there, uh, from around the yard around the apartments. That's where I buried it. I dug it up with my hand down into the dirt some.

In the follow-up interviews, Ronning went on to describe in greater detail when he first made contact with Maggie: "I opened the door to her bedroom. She got up...she had obviously been sleeping...she got up and said 'Hello.' And I ran across the bedroom and hit her and wrapped around her neck. Then she said 'I'll be nice.' And uh, we had sex. And uh...I killed her. She was wearing some type of nightee. Her bedroom was dark. There was a light on in the other room. It was night...seems like I remember a light being on in the living room but not the light overhead like a lamp off to the side or something."

Maggie's murder was not the only one to which Ronning confessed. He faced the video camera while recording his next confession, exposing a Grim Reaper tattoo on his arm and a stone cold expression on his face. He went into detail about the murder of Patricia Rosansky. "I had a gun...a starter pistol...I rolled down the window and she came over to the passenger side." Ronning got Rosansky into his car, went off a dirt road into a wooded area and forced her out of the car. "I made her take her clothes off, and I strangled her...I hit her in the head with a rock. Then I put a piece of, I think it was like a refrigerator door, or some kind of large sheet metal over her and uh, some other debris...and I left."

Ronning later confessed to the murder of Carrie Evans. He describes abducting Carrie by driving beside her as she walked to school, asked for directions and then raised a starter pistol to her face and ordered her into the car. He was unable to locate the crime scene when driven to the area. He claimed to have abducted her in the morning, although police reports noted that she was taken in the afternoon.

Regarding Patricia Rosansky, Ronning explained that he also used a starter pistol to scare the young girl into his car. He described how he led Patricia into the woods before raping and killing her by strangling her and then hitting her in the head with a rock. "I left her body nude." The most shocking part of the confession itself was Detective Mullen's own voice in the background, "We found her clothes folded; does that jog your memory?" Mullen constantly provided prompts along these lines in the confessions.

While Ronning's confessions seemed to hold some promise to a conviction, they were just too good to be true for prosecutors. The more Ronning talked, the more his stories just didn't line up. In the case of Maggie Hume, Michael Ronning was taken by bus back to Stringham Road to show where he had hidden Maggie's wallet. Flanked by police officers, he walked up to the side of the maintenance shed and said, "This looks like the area." He went on to describe burying the wallet in the dirt with his hands.

The discrepancies between Ronning's story and the physical evidence from the Maggie Hume case just kept adding up. First, Ronning described how he saw Maggie in the window from the bend in the road along the Kalamazoo River, where he was fishing. When you review the angle of her building, the distance and the approximate area where Ronning claimed he was fishing, it would have been impossible for him to have seen Maggie in the window. Additionally, all curtains and shades at the crime scene were drawn.

Ronning stated that his point of entry was from the balcony and into the apartment via the window. All officers at the crime scene agreed that all windows were secure and were not the point of entry at the time of offense—the door was. This was supported by the trail of grass clippings. The front door, by which Ronning said he left her apartment, was locked when Margaret returned at 3:45 a.m. from picking up her sister from the airport. The front door was only able to lock with a key or from the inside of the apartment. In short, Ronning's account of entry and exit to the apartment did not match the physical evidence at the crime scene.

Ronning's account noted that he startled Maggie in her sleep and that she stayed calm as she said, "Hello" and, "I'll be nice." No woman would wake up to a complete stranger in the middle of the night and be calm and inviting. Maggie would have never agreed to have sex with Ronning, even if it was "out of fear." In fact, without her glasses on, she would have likely seen a stranger in her apartment and would have screamed in response. Michael Ronning's account did not mention Maggie ever screaming out, yet her neighbors clearly heard it at about 2:00 a.m.

Ronning described how he strangled Maggie with the crook of his arm, but in fact the physical evidence and crime scene photographs clearly demonstrate that Maggie was strangled with a ligature object. Ronning described how he hit Maggie in the mouth/throat to confuse detectives regarding cause of death, but no such markings were seen on Maggie. Reports show that Maggie was intentionally sodomized, but Ronning claims that if there was anal contact, it was not done purposefully. In fact, in his account, he stated, "Uh, my wife informed me at one time that there was anal sex involved." Ronning's source was clearly identified in his testimony as Vicki Ronning. And where did she learn this information? It was never in the newspaper. One can only assume that in his investigation Dennis Mullen had revealed to Vicki Ronning this detail. Ronning would later testify in court that despite his divorce, he had probed his wife about any details that the police had provided her.

Ronning described how he left her purse on the dresser, but the purse was actually found near Maggie's body, almost under it.

Maggie's bed. The fitted sheet was pulled up at the corners. The pillow was wedged in at the headboard, which is where she usually put it when she and Jay had sex. Its position calls into question Carter's series of events. *Provided via FOIA, Battle Creek Police Department.*

Ronning also described covering Maggie's body with clothing pulled from the hangers in the closet. No empty hangers were found, and no clothes were used to cover the body up. The blanket, the only spare in the apartment, was located in the closet in the hallway, a place Ronning would not have known to look.

Living under Maggie and Margaret, Ronning would have likely known that Maggie had a roommate. If nothing else, the size and number of bedrooms in the apartment would have pointed to a roommate even if he never had seen her. Yet the physical evidence and the trail of grass clippings show that whoever came in from the balcony door did not even go to Margaret Van Winkle's bedroom to see if she was there. On any other night, Margaret would have been home, yet Michael Ronning seems to have disregarded any chance of her being present this night.

He also claimed to have taken her wallet and buried it on the curve of the roadway near the apartments. Ronning was unable to describe Maggie's wallet or purse and claimed that he never even looked inside the wallet. Michael Ronning was an admitted drug addict, so why didn't he check the wallet for money or take the uncashed check on the dining table?

The small dining area of apartment no. 19 as it appeared the day of the crime. *Provided via FOIA, Battle Creek Police Department.*

A close-up of the dining table shows an uncashed check in plain sight. A robber would have likely taken this. *Provided via FOIA, Battle Creek Police Department.*

Michael Ronning drew Detective Mullen a diagram of the victim's apartment. All two-bedroom apartments in the complex are laid out the exact same way. Ronning shared a two-bedroom apartment with his brother, Steve, and was obviously able to draw a diagram since they lived in the same complex. His drawing of Maggie's room did conform roughly to the photographs taken at the crime scene. As Joe Newman would later point out, the written police report was inaccurate, noting that Maggie's dresser was diagonally positioned, when it actually wasn't in the photographs. Either Ronning had a lucky guess or he hadn't fully memorized this portion of the investigators' report.

When asked about the shoes Ronning had been wearing the night of Maggie's murder, he described wearing a pair of tennis shoes. Detective Mullen seemed to think Ronning was wearing the pair of loafers that Vicki Ronning had described buying for her husband. Most likely, since Ronning had been fishing, he wouldn't have chosen to wear loafers to the river.

According to Dennis Mullen:

> *Well everything went to hell when Ted Hentchel got involved. He was Cress's attorney. When Ronning came up to confess, we didn't know it, but*

he called Hentchel and told him that he had just confessed to the Rosansky murder. The next Monday, Hentchel was in court filing a motion for a new trial for Cress. We always thought we'd have time to work all of this out. Once we got this taken care of and Ronning transferred, we could talk with other agencies and jurisdictions about other possible crimes. Ronning could then freely confess to other crimes. When Ted filed that motion, it put the Prosecutor's Office on the defense. Up until that point, we were working together. We should have had time to resolve this. That's when the sides were drawn. No one saw it—saw Ronning getting Hentchel involved. We thought we could have this done and done right, on the low key.

After having already gone to the local television media and engaging politicians to apply pressure to the Prosecutor's Office, the die had been cast by Mullen.

THE DEAL WITH THE DEVIL

You can give a man your whole heart and soul
But you cannot make him think
You could have been with me
Instead of alone and lonely...
        —"You Could Have Been with Me," Sheena Easton

Michael Ronning's confession seemed to forever intertwine the murder of Maggie Hume with the killings of Patricia Rosansky and Carrie Evans. While the three girls never met, Ronning's confessions in their deaths ignited a firestorm of lawsuits and court activity over the coming years.

His confession hung in the air for months in 1997–98. The most immediate effect was tied to the Patricia Rosansky case. While the court proceedings were centered on efforts to get Thomas Cress out of jail, they were as much about Maggie Hume as Patricia Rosansky. As such, an understanding of these cases, especially Ms. Rosansky's murder, is crucial.

Prior to Ronning's confession, the case against Thomas Cress seemed relatively solid. Seventeen-year-old Patricia Rosansky was reported missing on February 3, 1983. A junior at Battle Creek's Central High School, Patricia lived in the city with her brother and sister-in-law after the passing of her mother. She was enrolled in healthcare classes at the Community Center and was an active member of St. Philip Catholic Church. She was last seen at about 8:00 a.m. walking near Calhoun Street and North Avenue on her way to school. Patricia was with a friend that morning, and when her friend stopped to sneak a cigarette, she continued on alone. Within a block, she disappeared.

Several weeks later, Patricia's decomposed body was found covered in leaves and garbage in a steep, wooded ravine of Bedford Township near the Kalamazoo River by scrap collectors. An autopsy showed that the partially clothed petite teenager had been raped, sodomized and beaten to death, with her skull crushed. Tree limb pieces were found in Rosansky's throat.

Thomas Cress, a twenty-six-year-old mentally disabled man, was arrested in the summer of 1983 after an investigation by Michigan State and Bedford Township Police. The divorced father of three was described as a petty thief and frequent drinker and was known to smoke marijuana. He made a living by delivering newspapers and doing odd jobs such as custodial work and selling defective boxes of Kellogg's cereal. He couldn't read or write and had the mental capacity of an eight-year-old. Cress lived only a few doors down from Patricia Rosansky but claims that he barely knew her.

The Battle Creek Area Chamber of Commerce's Silent Observer program offered a $5,000 reward to the tipster who provided the information that led to Cress's arrest. Just days after that award was listed, six witnesses came forward stating that Thomas Cress had told them that he had killed Rosansky. Among those who had turned Cress in were Walter Moore, a jailed felon; his brother, Terry Moore; their sister-in-law, Candy Moore; and Candy's sister, Cindy Lesley. Their accounts told variants of the same story—that Cress admitted that he gave Patricia a ride, gave her marijuana and raped and killed her after she refused to have sex with him.

Cress, who took the stand during his trial, denied all allegations. He passed his polygraph test, and there was no physical evidence tying him to Patricia's murder. He had an alibi for the time of her disappearance—he had been delivering newspapers with a coworker, although his alibi witness could not account for him entirely during the time of the murder. Two other witnesses stepped forward during the trial. Shirley House testified that she overheard Cress say that he "had to kill the bitch" for sex. The other witness, Emery DeBruine, also overheard Cress in a bar state that he essentially killed Patricia because she had refused to have sex with him. During closing arguments, Calhoun County prosecutor Conrad Sindt explained to jurors that six witnesses had come forward to prove Cress was lying. In 1985, Cress was found guilty of killing Patricia Rosansky and sentenced to life in prison without the possibility of parole.

During the trial, there had been no physical evidence against Cress, just testimony about his admissions that he had killed Miss Rosansky. Despite what television and the movies portray, many murder convictions are based on circumstantial evidence, and at the time, it looked as if the case against

Cress was solid and tangible. Cress, like any man convicted of murder, appealed his case, but by the 1990s, he had exhausted all of his appeals. It appeared that he would remain in prison for his entire life.

On May 4, 1992, Jon Sahli received a routine "destroy all evidence" form from the Michigan State Police. The form explained that all of Thomas Cress's appeals had been exhausted and that evidence needed to be destroyed in order to make room in the state police storage facility. After reviewing the documentation, Sahli signed the document to destroy all physical evidence, including DNA evidence on a sanitary napkin, in the Rosansky case. It was a purely administrative procedure.

To Jon Sahli, there was no reason to retain the evidence since, to his knowledge, at the time, no one was investigating anything to do with the Rosansky case. Dennis Mullen had spoken with him about the Hume murder and that Ronning may confess to other murders in Michigan, but to his memory, the Cress/Rosansky case was never mentioned.

While the Rosansky case stole newspaper headlines and garnered considerable media attention, little mention was made about another missing girl at the same time, Carrie Evans. Evans was a seventeen-year-old junior at Bellevue High School, a town a few miles north of Battle Creek. She lived with her grandparents and played clarinet in the school band. In May 1983, her body was found buried under a pile of sticks in a wooded area behind the Sportsman's Club in Bellevue by mushroom hunters. She had been raped and presumably strangled. Miss Evans had been missing since March and was considered a "runaway." She was last seen walking down quiet Main Street of Bellevue, Michigan, on a Saturday afternoon. Unbeknownst to the authorities at the time, Michael Ronning had been living in the area at the time of her murder. In fact, he had taken the same road she had disappeared from while driving his sister, who he had custody of, to school.

No one had ever been charged in the murder of Carrie Evans. Her case had fallen into the jurisdiction of the Calhoun County Sheriff's Department and the state police. Unlike Patricia Rosansky, there seemed to be no public pressure to solve the case. It had happened in a tiny little town in the north end of Calhoun County, and despite dogged investigation, there were no apparent suspects.

Three young women—all killed when Michael Ronning was in the area and close to each of the victims. Two victims were concealed after death outdoors, while one was tucked into a closet. Two were abductions off the street. Two victims had been sodomized. Dennis Mullen saw connections, solidified in the form of Ronning's confession. The coincidences were too great to even consider that Michael Ronning might have lied.

Outside Ronning's confession to Patricia Rosansky's murder, two witnesses recanted their statements regarding Thomas Cress's involvement in the teenager's death. David Nickola, Thomas Cress's attorney, filed for a new trial after Ronning confessed to killing Patricia, setting off a flurry of legal activity. The circuit court granted Cress a new trial in 1997. Nancy Mullett of the Prosecutor's Office fought hard to keep Cress in jail, believing that Cress was still responsible for the murder. While two witnesses had recanted, she had deep concerns about Ronning's confession. And even if two witnesses had changed their testimony, there were still four others who swore that Thomas Cress had killed Patricia Rosansky.

Mullett is a spirited redheaded powerhouse. She graduated from Central Michigan University with a BS in education and from Wayne State University, Thomas M. Cooley Law School, with her JD, cum laude. She took her responsibility for protecting the community seriously. She and the Prosecutor's Office had sincere concerns about Ronning's confession.

First and foremost, Ronning could not find the murder scene when driven there. Dennis Mullen had taken him, with a video camera in tow, on a different approach to the scene. Mullen would claim that the area had changed a great deal, but Trooper Zimmerman, one of the original investigators on the case, demonstrated with crime scene photographs in court that the area had actually changed very little—in fact, some of the debris, such as a roof vent, were still there. But Ronning's description of where he killed Patricia Rosansky on the tape was flat-out wrong. She was found in a steep ravine, but Ronning indicated that she had been killed on a flat clearing area.

Furthermore, Michael Ronning's account of her demise was not consistent with the physical evidence. He claimed that he had strangled her and hit her with a rock once in the head. The medical experts disagreed, claiming that she had died as a result of multiple blows to the head and had been struck with an instrument consistent with a rod-like object. In fact, there was nothing that pointed to a strangulation. Ronning, in his videotaped confession, had stated that Patricia had been naked. In fact, she had been found partially clothed with her shirt, underpants and socks on.

Ronning's account of the abduction of Patricia Rosansky was bizarrely unbelievable. He claimed that he had convinced her to hop in a car with him, a total stranger, by threatening her with a starter pistol, yet she, at no point, offered any resistance to him. He claimed that they had sex in the back seat and smoked a joint. In his confession, his alleged victim had even giggled at one point. Ronning claimed that he strangled her without a struggle for four minutes, hitting her head with a rock afterward. In reality, Patricia had fought her killer. Her mitten had been found in the mud, sunk in as if she had battled her assailant as she wrestled on the ground—none of which was in Ronning's statements.

This was not Nancy Mullett's first exposure to Ronning's confessions:

> *In the 1990s, early on, Joe Newman and Denny Mullen approached me. We met over at the courthouse, which I thought was weird because we usually met in my office. They said they trusted me. They asked me to look at the Ronning confessions and at the evidence in the three cases. They wanted my opinion. It took me a long time to review it all. I told them that the same person did not kill the three of them. For sure, Michael Ronning didn't kill Maggie Hume. If anything, a review of the evidence pointed clearly to Jay Carter. I found even more evidence that Cress might have been tied in some way to the Evans murder—it turns out he hung out at the gun club where her body was found.*

What made the court cases tied to Cress/Rosansky even more divisive was the fact that Detective Mullen was brought forth as the key defense witness. "The problem was that Denny tended to make a decision then jammed all of the evidence into it. I was stunned when I showed up for the Cress hearings and they were there as witnesses for the defense. Denny is a good guy, so is Joe [Newman]. Denny has just lost his perspective…he was unwilling to entertain alternate explanations. He just got all caught up in this stuff. I mean here I was at a hearing on the Cress matter, with the judge from Jackson, and there he is as the primary witness."

Former prosecutor Jon Sahli became the focus of court proceedings as well. His destruction of evidence was alleged to have been done to protect the conviction of Thomas Cress. The thinking was that with new DNA analysis, a sanitary napkin with sperm on it recovered from Patricia Rosansky's remains might have proven Thomas Cress innocent—had that evidence been deliberately destroyed? These proceedings became more of a glimpse into Dennis Mullen's investigation techniques than any deliberate action that Sahli was accused of doing. Jon Sahli testified that he first heard of the connection of Ronning to the Rosansky murder in either the summer of 1994 or 1995. This was substantiated with his notes at the time and witnesses. Both Dennis Mullen and Joe Newman testified against the former prosecutor. While their own notes did not substantiate their claims, they pointed out that often meetings were held where notes were not taken.

A procession of former and subsequent prosecutors was arranged to testify that Mullen had no jurisdiction to even look into the Rosansky and Evans cases. They claimed that Dennis Mullen had only been focused on the murder of Maggie Hume until just before Ronning's confessions. In fact, officers tied to the Rosansky case said they had not talked to Mullen about the murder until after the evidence had been destroyed. John Hallacy, who was an assistant prosecutor in 1992, didn't remember Mullen discussing Rosansky until 1995 or 1996, long after the evidence was destroyed.

Up until 1994, all supporting notes from Battle Creek Police Department and the Prosecutor's Office indicated that all discussions around Michael Ronning were only associated with the Maggie Hume murder case. According to Sahli in his testimony, no assistant prosecutor was ever penalized for losing a case. When asked, "Did you ever imply to them there would be problems if they lost a case?" he responded, "No." The implication was that there was not a culture to preserve prosecutions.

Assistant Prosecutor Matthew Glaser remembered a meeting in August 1992 (after the evidence had been destroyed) during which the plan to move Ronning to Michigan was discussed. "It was all Maggie Hume. There wasn't—I don't remember any other homicide until later on, but then he was gonna plead to Maggie Hume." When asked if Dennis Mullen had ever expressed any belief to Glaser that Ronning was responsible for other murders other than Maggie Hume, Glaser said, "Through the core—well, yeah. Mullen, in the beginning, primarily when Jon would have been involved that I recall he would just list names and/or something he might have said locations of the murders, but there was large numbers and the numbers changed quite frequently. I mean there was a significant number—at one point I think there was probably 25 or 30 that were suspected."

The allegation that Jon Sahli had covertly destroyed evidence that might free a convicted man, even on the surface, seemed laughable. Conrad Sindt, the former prosecutor, had tried Thomas Cress originally. Another prosecutor, John Hallacy, was in the office at that time of the charges against Sahli. They had all won elections to put one another in office against their rivals. There would have been no reason for Sahli to try and preserve the conviction of a predecessor's actions. As Nancy Mullett put it years later, "Trust me, John Sahli has a lot of issues, but he *never* would have knowingly destroyed evidence if he knew Mullen and Newman were pursuing an investigation into Ronning being tied to the Rosansky case."

Nancy Mullett drove the point home in her summary to the court:

> *Denny Mullen and Newman were asked repeatedly why don't you go up to the Michigan State Police? At one point, I believe Newman said he didn't believe it was appropriate; that it would be inappropriate without the permission of the prosecutor. That didn't make sense. Conrad Sindt said it was absolutely not his obligation to give them permission, in fact, never was. And it's very difficult, I would imagine, for this court to believe that the Battle Creek Police Department believed they needed permission to go to another agency to talk about that agency's case. And it's very difficult I would imagine for this court to believe that even if that was the tenor of Conrad Sindt's office that in the face of this they would have followed up and not gone to the original agency. They contacted Denny Mullen—at least from his testimony [from] numerous jurisdictions. Numerous police agencies throughout the United States talking to them about his belief that Michael Ronning killed someone in their jurisdiction. He talked to them. He corresponded. Apparently he compared notes with California. He went to Texas. He went to Florida. He did not go two miles to the Battle Creek Police Post on Columbia Avenue. He could have, but he didn't and I don't know why. I can speculate. I can theorize. He had a serial killer, plain and simple. He hit the big one. Finally, after all his years of coming back empty handed. He finally got a serial killer and if he went to the Michigan State Police the control would be lost, it would not be his case any longer.*

Dennis Mullen, years later, viewed his reluctance to go to the Michigan State Police very differently: "You know the prosecutors made a big deal about, 'Why didn't you get the other jurisdictions involved if you were working their cases?' But aren't they considered the chief law enforcement officers for the county where those jurisdictions were? They said you should have done it—gotten them involved. What about them? Isn't it their responsibility to do that?" Mullen felt that he had been painted as a "crooked cop." In reality, having reviewed the testimonies, it looked more as if Mullen was caught up with the thought of capturing a serial killer and/or he had been simply manipulated by Michael Ronning.

The courts agreed with Nancy Mullett and ruled that Sahli had *not* destroyed the evidence maliciously, but in many respects the damage had been done. All that this sideline did was to further widen the rift between the Prosecutor's Office and the Battle Creek Police Department.

The decision was appealed in 1999 to the Michigan Court of Appeals. Cress was then awarded a new trial after it was reversed on an appeal. Nancy Mullett moved in the trial court to reopen the proofs regarding Cress's motion for a new trial. The prosecutor sought to present the new evidence attacking the veracity of Ronning's confession. The trial court granted the prosecutor's motion. This shifted the focus away from Thomas Cress and on just how valid Michael Ronning's account he had provided police was.

At the hearing, several prosecution witnesses testified that Ronning had told them that he falsely confessed to the victim's murder. Members of Ronning's own family testified against him on the stand. Ronning was Melissa Meyer's guardian, and she maintained contact with him while he was incarcerated. She testified that he had admitted to her that he had indeed committed the Arkansas murder for which he was imprisoned. He also told her that his goal was to do time in Michigan and that he had *not* committed the murder of Patricia Rosansky. Melissa also testified that Ronning told her that he had obtained information from the secretary of his Michigan attorney, had read some transcripts of the court proceedings in the matter and had attempted to memorize facts related to the crimes. Melissa Meyer also testified that Michael Ronning is "a very intelligent and very manipulative person." Ronning had confessed to his half-sister, Rebecca Benning, that he had lied about the Rosansky murder to be transferred to a Michigan prison to avoid hard labor and to be closer to his family.

This was as critical to the Rosansky murder case as it was to Maggie Hume's. It calls into question the motivations of Michael Ronning and how he used information provided him to provide a handful of details in his confessions that were never made public before.

The court documents note, "Perhaps the most compelling evidence which causes this Court to conclude that Mr. Ronning is a false confessor comes from Mr. Ronning himself. In April 1997, Detective Mullen and others had Ronning attempt to show them where the scene of the crime was while being videotaped." Ronning identified the area of the crime scene on a flat piece of ground, a clearing next to a two-track without any landmarks. Photographs and other evidence show that Rosansky was found in a ravine, not a flat area. After comparing Ronning's recollection of the crime scene to the videotaped confession and the videotaped location Ronning identified, "the only reasonable conclusion one can draw is that Mr. Ronning didn't know where the crime scene was because he did not commit the crime."

Michael Ronning was put on the stand for the first time to be cross-examined on one of his confessions. Ronning testified that he killed Patricia

Rosansky but refused to answer any questions about the circumstances of the murder, claiming that to do so would somehow violate his agreement with the government. Nancy Mullett pointed out that Ronning's confessions to the murder of Rosansky have never been given under oath or with the benefit of cross-examination. The Calhoun County Prosecutor's Office required that Ronning submit to and pass a polygraph examination. The polygraph examiner's written report concluded that Ronning had voluntarily participated and truthfully acknowledged committing three murders in Michigan, but it didn't indicate *which* three murders:

> *The trial court further rejected its prior reliance on Detective Mullen's opinion that Ronning killed the victim, nothing other than police agencies and detectives disagreed with Mullen that Ronning killed three young women in Michigan, including the victim. The trial court also found it significant that Mullen did not investigate the victim's murder, speak with the State Police who had initially investigated the victim's murder, read the defendant's trial transcript, or speak with witnesses from defendant's trial or with defendant himself before reaching the conclusion that Ronning killed Rosansky. Detective Mullen's opinion that Mr. Ronning committed the Rosansky murder is based primarily upon his professional opinion and instinct, as opposed to any newly-discovered facts or evidence obtained during the course of his investigation.*

The trial court vacated its December 1997 decision and denied the defendant's motion for a new trial because it "no longer believes that a different result at a re-trial is probable." The court explained that it no longer found Ronning's confession persuasive.

Furthermore, during direct examination of Detective Dennis Mullen, the detective himself explained how he had given Michael Ronning information, including Maggie Hume's name, date of birth, description of her physical appearance, the location of where her body was found, manner of death and time of death. It was even brought up in the courtroom that Detective Mullen had given Ronning indirect clues during the time Ronning was taken to locate the Rosansky crime scene. As one witness, a jailhouse informant, said, Ronning was manipulating Mullen, who was "helping him pinpoint the place and playing hot and cold."

Matters got even more complicated when the national news media was dragged into the Michael Ronning confession as it related to Maggie Hume's murder. On February 1, 2002, *Dateline NBC* ran an episode titled "True Lies," featuring Stone Phillips covering the Michael Ronning story. In the episode, Michael Ronning described himself as a serial killer but wouldn't state how many homicides he committed.

Mullen and Newman took on the roles of the lone honest police officers battling against a corrupt Prosecutor's Office that was determined to keep an innocent man in jail. They were flown to New York to meet with the producers of the show. Mullen appeared on the episode, reinforcing his belief that Ronning was a serial killer.

In Michael Ronning's own words from the *Dateline* episode, "I'm not an honest person. In other words, I lie all the time." The episode focuses on the fact that Jon Sahli was believed to have had the Rosansky evidence destroyed in order to keep the conviction on Thomas Cress. Ronning explained that his confession could have cleared a lot of cases, but he felt that no one believed him. When asked if Ronning would answer questions in other states, he said, "Everybody that was supposedly behind me and helping me out, abused and abandoned me out there, left me standing in the middle of the room by myself. Now, you think I want to go in there—into agreements with another state and have the same thing happen again? There is no way."

Detective Mullen stated that he believes Ronning is responsible for "25 or 40—or more" murders. Ronning answered differently: "Not even close; far less. There's seven total. That's all I'll say. I won't say what states or anything else." Ronning gave a "no comment" and denied knowing either of the girls who went missing and were found near each other in Texas.

Stone Phillips acknowledged that the shoes that Vicki Ronning stated Michael Ronning owned matched the shoe print left on Maggie's balcony. He further demonstrated that Michael Ronning could have climbed up to the balcony and into the window, as he described in the confession. With Dennis Mullen as a guide, the story presented was that Ronning had provided a confession that had some details in it that were plausible in the murder of Maggie Hume.

What was missing was the Prosecutor's Office offering any sort of rebuttal with the physical evidence. It declined to be party to the interview, still harboring that the evidence it was withholding might still be usable in pursuing a case against Jay. As Nancy Mullett recounted, "I showed up one day back from lunch, and Stone Phillips was in my office. He knew a *lot* of the information, information we never released on the case. He asked me my opinion, and I didn't answer him. 'Look, you don't have a story unless you support Ronning's claim that he killed these three women. So whatever I say will be contrary to your story.' When Stone Phillips climbed up there

The balcony door was the point of entrance for the murderer. *Provided via FOIA, Battle Creek Police Department.*

on the balcony and proved you could enter the window—well, that was not accurate at all. The interior was laid out totally different than it was the day of the crime. It just couldn't have happened that way."

Maggie's mother, Lorie, was also featured on the show. "I just don't understand the prosecution's hesitation, and that's frustrating." John Hume also stated in the show that he believed that Ronning was the man who killed his sister and that there was enough evidence to charge and convict Ronning in her murder.

The Hume family had become unwitting pawns in the struggle between the Battle Creek Police Department and the Prosecutor's Office. As Jeff Kabot of the Prosecutor's Office put it, "That was part of the problem of the discord with the Police Department and us. Nancy Mullett talked to Maggie's mom with me. We laid out the 'who and why'—in terms of it being Jay Carter. By the time we were finished, she agreed that Jay had killed Maggie." In the public eye, however, Ronning still appeared a viable suspect.

With the Michigan Supreme Court ruling against Thomas Cress's appeals for a new trial, the matter lay dormant for some time. The Michigan Innocence Project got involved with his cause. On the surface, it looked as if the Calhoun County Prosecutor's Office was fighting hard to keep an innocent man (Thomas Cress) in prison when it had a perfectly good confession in hand. The news media fell into this thinking, mostly because the Prosecutor's Office never revealed all of the flaws with Ronning's confessions since two of the cases, Hume and Evans, were still open investigations. The trial got bumped to the Supreme Court, where Nancy Mullett argued that Cress shouldn't get a new trial, citing that the lower courts had ruled Michael Ronning "a false confessor." The justices agreed and denied a new trial for Thomas Cress. The Michigan Innocence Project continued to press the matter. On her last days in office, in December 2010, Michigan governor Granholm commuted Cress's sentence.

The aftermath of the release of Thomas Cress was a blow to the Prosecutor's Office, which had won its cases up to the Michigan Supreme Court and had Michael Ronning labeled as a false confessor.

The members of the Rosansky family were devastated. The man they believed to have killed their beloved Patricia was now free in society. Although he was transferred directly from prison to a mental hospital, he was later released into society on parole. Nancy Mullett still believes that Thomas Cress is Patricia's murderer. Dennis Mullen and Joe Newman are passionate in their belief that Michael Ronning is Patricia's murderer.

With Michael Ronning tagged as a "false confessor," he was sent back to do "hard time" in an Arkansas prison at his own request. He was never charged with any of the crimes to which he confessed in Michigan. Detective Mullen and Newman still believe that Ronning is responsible for not only those murders but also many unsolved homicides throughout the United States. At one point, Detective Mullen believed that Ronning was responsible for some of the Green River murders and upward of twenty murders overall.

WHAT WAS LOST IN ALL of this was the implication for Ronning's confession for Maggie's murder. In Dennis Mullen's mind, the three confessions were tied together. "There's some difficulty in accepting [Ronning's] confession on the Hume case and not on the others. Our deal with him was not driven by numbers [of murders]. If they accepted on one case, they had to clear Cress on the Rosansky murders."

Prosecutors disagree. Jon Sahli, former prosecutor for Calhoun, never believed Michael Ronning's confession in the Hume case. He explained in an interview:

> *Everything he said in his confession was easily obtainable through the police reports or the media. I gave that confession the same consideration that I would give to any other piece of evidence presented to me during the course of a criminal investigation. Ultimately, based upon everything I knew of the case, I came to the conclusion that Mr. Ronning's confession was false and should not be considered. I told Mr. and Mrs. Hume that, in my opinion, making a deal with Michael Ronning was like making a deal with the devil himself. I also expressed to them my feeling that it was in Mr. Ronning's best interests to have a First Degree Murder Conviction in the State of Michigan in the hopes he would be incarcerated here in Michigan rather than in Arkansas. The reason for his preference in serving a sentence in Michigan is that prisoners within the Michigan Department of Corrections, to my understanding, are free to determine whether or not they wish to work in one of the state run facilities during their time of incarceration or pursue weight lifting or some other form of entertainment. This needs to be contrasted with the southern method of performing physical labor from five in the afternoon six days a week. Couple this with the fact that Michael Ronning's family was in Michigan and could visit him if he were able to be incarcerated in this state. Given these facts it would appear to me that Michigan would be the preferable place to spend the rest of your life locked up.*

Ronning, for his part, lobbied to be returned to Arkansas to serve out his sentence. As Dennis Mullen remembered it, "Michael was being jerked around by the prosecutors. I was on his side…I wanted them to throw the switch [on accepting his confession]. But it was frustrating. In the end, they just sent him back." At the time of this writing, Michael Ronning remains in an Arkansas prison, where he will remain until the end of his natural life.

What everyone can agree on is the strained relations between the Battle Creek Police Department and the Calhoun County Prosecutor's Office. But where did this rift begin? Was it the prosecutors' attempt to protect the conviction of Thomas Cress? No. It began with two officers who went to the media, politicians and so on, to press an agenda of closing the Maggie Hume case on a highly questionable confession. It played out in courts, on national television and with lawmakers on Capitol Hill, where Carl Levin pressed for a bill that would retain capital crimes evidence for one hundred years. It *did* result in the release of Thomas Cress, but it did not clear him of the murder of Patricia Rosansky.

The ramifications in the rift between the Battle Creek Police Department and the Calhoun County Prosecutor's Office ran deep. As Jon Sahli has conveyed:

> I believe that Virgil Jay Carter was the likely suspect in the matter, but the only other person in law enforcement that seemed to be of that opinion was Detective Alan Tolf of the Battle Creek City Police Department. It seemed to me that the Battle Creek City Police Department had not spent much, if any time, investigating him as a suspect as it was apparent to me that no one in the department, with the possible exception of Detective Tolf, would be willing to back a prosecution of Carter. In short, it is my opinion that the main players in this case from the Battle Creek Police Department had concluded that Michael Ronning committed all three of these murders within Calhoun County and there was nothing that myself or anyone else could do or say to persuade them otherwise.

Is Michael Ronning a serial killer? Maybe. He most certainly is a manipulative individual and is a convicted murderer. Does that mean he killed Maggie Hume? There are severe issues with his confession that cannot be ignored. Was this the story of two officers who were the sole bastions of justice…or two officers who had gotten too close to the case? Was there a grand conspiracy between three or four generations of prosecutors to bury and suppress the truth and ignore three confessions? No, the courts ruled on that. In the end, the bitter infighting certainly mauled the career of Dennis Mullen and cast extreme doubt as to whether anyone would ever be charged in the murder of Maggie Hume.

But with the changing of prosecutors and leaders in the police department, new eyes fell on the Hume case and, with them, the glimmer of hope that charges will be one day made.

THE FINAL TWO SUSPECTS

I never meant to be so bad to you
One thing I said that I would never do
One look from you and I would fall from grace
And that would wipe this smile right from my face.
— *"Heat of the Moment," Asia*

In the end, after more than three decades of political bickering, mangled careers and slanted media coverage, there are two primary suspects in the murder of Maggie Hume: Michael Ronning and Virgil Jay Carter.

Sure, there were other potential suspects—like Thomas Strong, Tom Carpenter and Jim Downey—but inevitably there is nothing tangible that provides a good motive or means for any of them to have committed the crime. Jim Downey was quite helpful with authorities and eventually cleared by polygraph. His only "crime" was remaining good friends with a former girlfriend, nothing more or less. He never had a tangible motive for murdering Maggie other than an alleged abortion, and that is flimsy at best. Strong, while an obstinate and questionable handyman, never could be linked to the crime. Other than deliberately skewing his polygraph exam, he was little more than a distraction for investigators. Tom Carpenter was more than forthcoming, and his only paper-thin motive might be the loss of a part-time minimum wage job.

These three men were looked at by seasoned investigators and ruled out for good reasons. In the end, only two men remain standing in the wings as potential killers. The confessor, Michael Ronning, and Jay Carter. For each, we will look at the case for and against them, leaving it for you, the reader, to make your own judgment call.

Michael Ronning

With Michael Ronning, the issue a person must grapple with is simple yet complex: "Is Michael Ronning a serial killer?" If you can accept that as true, you can pry open the case against him. Or was Michael Ronning simply, as the courts eventually ruled, manipulating investigators to fulfill his own personal needs?

In the end, his credibility hangs entirely on his confession that he murdered Maggie Hume. So, analyzing that confession becomes important in whether you are willing to accept him as her murderer. Was his memory of that night in August 1982 blurred by his use of drugs, or was he simply never there?

Factors Pointing Toward Ronning as the Murderer

- Ronning willingly confessed to Maggie Hume's murder, as well as to the murders of Carrie Evans and Patricia Rosansky.
- Michael Ronning is clearly violent, with some tendencies that might point to him being a serial killer. One interview said that he enjoyed torturing animals as a child. Another report mentions him going after a female family member with a hammer. Yet another said that he got angry enough to hit a co-worker with a 2x4 plank on a construction site.
- Ronning was a criminal. He served time in the state prison for burglary and stealing cars. He was arrested in the late 1970s for attempted rape and armed robbery in California, as well as indecent exposure in Oregon and suspicion of raping a drugged prostitute in California.
- Ronning openly admits to being a drug addict and admits to using cocaine the night of Maggie's murder. The use of drugs potentially could have altered Ronning's state of mind and recollection.
- Ronning has been convicted of the murder of Diana Henley.
- Ronning had stalking tendencies. Ronning's former boss, Darryl Meredith, reported to police that Ronning had stalked a young

teenage girl in a convenience store and had verbally stated that he wanted to track her down and have sex with her. There is no evidence, however, that he stalked Maggie Hume, and he did not confess to that.

- He lived in the exact same apartment complex as Maggie Hume at the time of her murder.
- Ronning was unaccounted for during the time of Maggie's murder. He had left his apartment at 11:30 p.m., telling his wife that he was going fishing.
- Mike and Vicki Ronning left abruptly for Texas the day after Maggie's murder. In fact, Angie Henson, a roommate of Mike's, did not even tell police that Michael Ronning was an occupant of the apartment upon being interviewed by investigators. It should be noted, however, that he had planned to leave that day several days in advance.
- If you subscribe to the concept of Ronning as a serial killer, he *may* be possibly linked to other murders in other states such as Texas and California. All these murders occurred while Ronning was in each area. At best, his presence is an awkward coincidence. It should be noted that he has never been charged in any of these crimes.
- At a New Years Eve party on the last day of 1982, Ronning was questioned by a partygoer regarding his possible involvement in the Maggie Hume murder. Ronning neither confirmed or denied this question, instead he just grinned and looked away.
- Vicki Ronning picked out from a 1982 Sears catalogue a pair of loafers that Michael had often worn in 1982. The specific brand of the shoe and the sole were compared to the shoe prints left on the utility box outside Maggie's apartment. If her memory was correct, the soles and size were a match, possibly linking Ronning directly to Maggie's apartment.
- Ronning himself asked to take a polygraph regarding crimes in Michigan. He tested positive for admitting to killing three people in Michigan but not Maggie Hume specifically.
- Ronning accurately described the location where Maggie Hume's wallet was found.
- Ronning was able to accurately describe the general layout of Maggie's bedroom.
- Ronning was able to accurately state that Maggie Hume's cause of death was strangulation.

Factors Pointing Away from Ronning as the Murderer

- Although the shoe print matched the shoes Vicki Ronning had claimed Ronning wore the night of Maggie's murder, Michael Ronning insisted in his taped confession that he was wearing tennis shoes the night of the murder. Ronning's version makes more sense. He claimed that he was fishing the night of Maggie's death; it would make more sense that Ronning was wearing tennis shoes to go fishing instead of the loafers that Vicki Ronning claimed he was wearing. While most of us might be hard-pressed to remember what shoes we wore on a particular night a year ago, Vicki Ronning is mysteriously able to remember the shoes that her former husband wore on a specific night more than a decade later—something that is highly suspect. And the shoes in question have long since been destroyed, leaving us with a *story* about a possible pair of shoes.
- Vicki Ronning, per Dennis Mullen, may not be reliable for the same reason that Michael's memory might be tainted. "She was a crack addict and was screwing a motorcycle gang when I found her."
- Although Ronning offered to take a polygraph, and "passed," the questions asked during the polygraph examination were very vague and did not include any details. We don't know which three murders he may have actually committed, and Maggie's may not have been one of them.
- Keith Hall also testified that Mullen had told him "everything about the murders" and that he was permitted to look through police files. Detective Mullen later testified in court that he did indeed share information concerning the open homicide cases with Keith Hall. Detective Mullen also testified in court that he had given Michael Ronning information including Maggie Hume's name, date of birth, general physical description, the location of where her body was found, manner of death and time of death and the location of her wallet. This gave Ronning access to details of the crime that would have effectively invalidated his entire confession to Maggie's murder.
- Ronning's confession to the murder of Patricia Rosansky was proven in court to be a fabrication. He was unable to accurately describe the correct location of Patricia Rosansky's body and claimed that Patricia was found "nude." In reality, Patricia was clothed with a sweater, underwear and socks on. He also described hitting her once in the head with a rock. After her body was exhumed, it was

discovered that Patricia was hit more than once in the head with a blunt object. Patricia's body was also found with sticks lodged in her throat, a very unique and significant finding in a homicide. Ronning

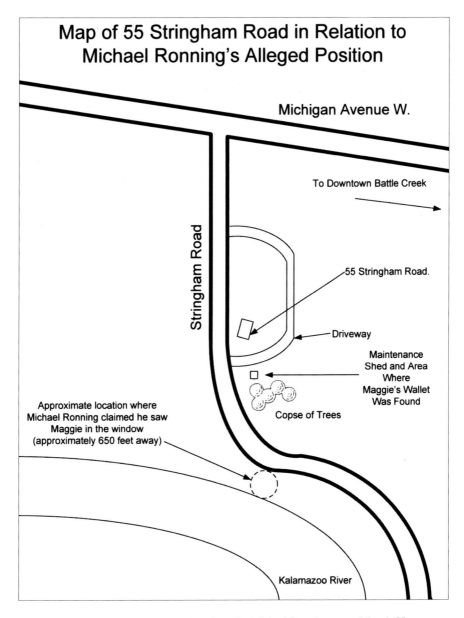

A map showing how difficult it would have been for Michael Ronning to see Maggie Hume on the night of the murder. It would have been almost impossible. *Created by Blaine Pardoe.*

did not describe any such act. Likewise, in his confession to Carrie Evans's murder, Ronning stated that he picked up the young girl while she was walking on her way to school. In reality, Carrie Evans did not disappear until later in the afternoon.

- Michael Ronning described seeing Maggie Hume from the river bend while fishing on the night of her murder. After further investigation and a visit to the site, it was found to be impossible to see into Maggie's apartment from the distance and location of the river bend at which Mike claimed to be fishing. If he couldn't see Maggie at the window (where the curtains were drawn), he would have had no reason to initiate his attack on her.

- Ronning stated that his point of entry into Maggie's apartment was through climbing up onto the balcony and then climbing through the window by removing the screen. While Ronning stated that he is very skilled at climbing, the officers at the scene of the crime agreed that all windows were secure and intact. The point of entry was the door from the balcony, as evidenced by it being unlocked and there being grass clippings leading from the door and into Maggie's bedroom.

- Per his confession, at no point did Ronning check to see if her roommate was home, so he had no idea that she was alone that evening. A person planning to murder someone would usually check for any potential witnesses or anyone else in the apartment who could divert the murder or call for help. Living under the victim, Ronning would have likely been aware that she had a roommate, but he never checked to see if she was at home.

- Ronning stated that he left via the front door of the apartment. The lock on the front door of Maggie and Margaret's apartment is only able to lock from the inside. Margaret, upon her return to the apartment at 3:45 a.m., stated the front door was indeed locked.

- When Ronning described startling Maggie in her sleep, he stated that she greeted him with, "Hello" and, "I'll be nice." No one would wake up to an intruder in their bedroom and be so calm and cooperating. This is illogical given the circumstances.

- Maggie could not see without her glasses. Ronning does not describe her putting on her glasses when he enters her room. Maggie would not have even known who was in her room in the darkness, so her reaction would have been even more terrified.

- In his confession, Ronning stated that he grabbed Maggie around the throat and hit her. No markings indicated that she was grabbed by the throat. Maggie was strangled with a ligature, which is supported by her autopsy. Ronning's account did not match the physical evidence.

- Ronning went on to state that he kicked Maggie in the neck several times to conceal the fact that she was strangled. No postmortem markings or bruising were found to be consistent with Ronning's statements.

- Ronning described having sex with Maggie and that she "consented probably out of fear." Maggie Hume was a relatively conservative Catholic who did not enjoy sex even with her boyfriend and would have never agreed to willingly have sex with a complete stranger.

- Ronning described the sodomy with his alleged victim: "My wife informed me at one time that there was anal sex involved. If that's true, it was inadvertent." This statement proves that Ronning was only aware of the traumatic anal sex via the information that his wife gave him. This detail was never made public in the newspapers. Vicki Ronning could have only obtained that information from Dennis Mullen—opening the question as to just how much information about the case Vicki Ronning may have been exposed to and leaked to Michael.

- Ronning described how he left Maggie's purse on the dresser. Her purse was later recovered near her body in the closet.

- In his confession, he stated that he took her wallet from the purse and buried it under leaves and dirt on the curve of the roadway near the apartments. Although the wallet was later found in this general area, Ronning was unable to describe either the wallet or the purse. This location could easily have been obtained from police reports to which he had access.

- Ronning stated himself that he was a drug addict. Drug addicts require money in order to keep up with their supply to feed their addiction; Ronning took Maggie's wallet without even looking inside to see if it contained any money.

- While Ronning was able to accurately draw a layout of Maggie's bedroom, the apartment complex's two-bedroom apartments were all laid out exactly the same way, making it easy for Ronning to draw an accurate layout.

- Michael Ronning had no motive to murder Maggie Hume. He stated that he broke into her apartment strictly to kill her.

- While he may have had little to no motive to kill any of the victims he confessed to killing, Ronning did have a motive to confess overall.

Not only would he be transferred to a prison in Michigan and avoid further mandatory hard labor in Arkansas, but he would also avoid being charged with any other murders in other states that used the death penalty. Not to mention Michael Ronning has family in Michigan who would most likely have visited him in prison.

- Melissa Meyer, Michael Ronning's younger sister, of whom he once had custody, stated that Ronning told her that it was his goal to do time in Michigan and that he had read transcripts and memorized facts regarding the murders to which he confessed. She also testified that Michael Ronning is a "very intelligent person and very manipulative."
- In 1997, Michigan's courts labeled Michael Ronning as a "false confessor."
- Jon Sahli, former prosecutor of Calhoun County, stated, "Everything he said in his confessions were easily obtainable through police reports or the media."
- Not a bit of physical evidence exists to support Michael Ronning ever having been in the victim's apartment.
- In Michael Ronning's own words, "I'm not an honest person. In other words, I lie all the time."

VIRGIL JAY CARTER

It must be pointed out that the case against Jay Carter is mostly circumstantial evidence. Television shows and movies cloud our thinking about murders. We tend to think that there's always some CSI-discovered evidence that convicts a killer. In reality, most murder cases are won not on the physical evidence but on a solid string of circumstantial evidence. In the case of Maggie Hume, for example, DNA testing would not have helped against Jay since he admitted to having sex with the victim the night she died.

With the notable exceptions of Dennis Mullen and Joe Newman, every other investigator associated with the death of Maggie Hume felt that Jay was her killer (including the cold case team in 2000). As Detective Al Tolf conveyed, "This is basically a boyfriend/girlfriend murder—plain and simple." Many times, the simple solutions are the ones proven to be the most credible.

With Jay, there are things that investigators simply don't know. For example, did Jay actually leave Maggie's apartment that night, or did he remain, kill her and return later via the balcony to conceal her body? Did he confess his involvement with the crime to Terry Sheerer and Bart Thiessen?

Factors Pointing Toward Carter as the Murderer

- Jay Carter was the last person to see her alive. While on its own that doesn't make a substantive difference, as Detective Tolf explained, "Usually the first person you want to pull in is the last person that sees the victim. You do this to see if their story holds water." In the case of Jay Carter, there were issues from the very start.
- His timeline of events the evening of the crime was difficult to reconcile. Ultimately, the question remains: why would he lie about the events prior to Maggie's death if not to throw off investigators?
- There was no evidence of a problem with Maggie's car; Jay incorporated this into his version of events leading up to her death.
- The day Maggie went missing, Jay claims to have gone to St. Phil to look for Mr. Hume, yet no one saw him in a school almost devoid of students. Why?
- Jay gave inconsistent descriptions of the call that came in from Jim Downey to Maggie—as if he were trying to implicate the caller as being responsible for her death. He told John Hume that the caller said "some crude things he wanted to do to Maggie." He told the police minutes earlier that the call was not an obscene call but rather was more of a nuisance. Why create that element of the story except to draw attention away from himself?
- If Jay believed that the caller was any possible threat to his girlfriend, why didn't he spend the night with Maggie—on a night when he alone knew that she would be alone?
- When John Hume and Jay went to the apartment, Jay was seen by John Hume on his knees at the floor of the closet where Maggie's body was found, claiming to be looking for shoes. It would have been impossible to look for the shoes without finding Maggie's legs. Jay contended that he didn't see Maggie there, but detectives and photographs show the legs partially exposed to even see her shoes. In addition to this, Jay admitted to investigators that he knew the

Snuggle Sack was out of place—it should have drawn his attention but apparently didn't.

- In Battle Creek on the night of the murder, there were only two people who knew that Maggie would be home alone that night: Jay and the victim. On any other night, the murderer would have surprised Margaret Van Winkle at home. The killer entered the apartment via the balcony door and went straight to Maggie's room and then left, leaving a trail of freshly cut grass clippings. No one even checked to see if Margaret was in her room. Maggie's killer remained in the apartment for a while, taking money from her purse to make it look like a burglary, wrapping the body and putting it in the tight confines of the closet. Whoever murdered Maggie knew that there was time to do all of these activities before her roommate came home.

- The body was concealed in such a way as to demonstrate some degree of guilt, pointing to a person who knew the victim. Only someone who had feelings for the victim would have taken the time and care to bundle the victim in such a manner in the closet.

- There was only one extra blanket in the apartment, and Maggie was covered with it in the closet, pointing to someone who knew where it was kept.

- Whoever left her apartment after killing her left via the balcony door. Jay would have known that the apartment door would not have been able to be locked if he had left via the door.

- Jay had been seen by at least three people choking Maggie at St. Phil at a volleyball game months prior to the murder. One witness heard Carter say that he "was going to put her in a dark place where nobody would find her," and her body was found months later in a closet. While he denied ever going to the games, John Hume said that he was there, and he was identified by someone who knew him personally: Sheila Guerra.

- Jay, who had a tendency to stay with his girlfriend when presented with the opportunity, left her on the one night when she was alone and when *she* asked *him* if he would be spending the night.

- Jay expressed to Maggie's friends and family that she had been raped. That information was not released even to the family until two weeks later.

- Maggie's pillow was between the bed and the wall, where she usually put it when she had sex with Carter. This is inconsistent with his account of their intercourse that evening.

- Jay commented to members of the Hume family that he "knew they [the murderer] cared about her cuz they wrapped and covered her so neatly and carefully with Snuggle-Sack." He also confided that "whoever killed Maggie must have loved her." He said, "It was an accident." Jay told Mr. Hume that Maggie was so neatly wrapped and her head turned in such a way that it had to have been done with care. Some of these comments point to potential guilt on his part. Others reveal information that Jay had no access to, such as the tilting of her head.

- His reaction during the period leading up to the funeral was to stay away from the Hume family. Jay also tried to ask out Mary Landstra only a few days after Maggie's death—hardly behavior consistent with someone in mourning.

- Jay had demonstrated a violent temper before in front of witnesses. In fact, most people who knew Maggie and Jay pointed to the tumultuous and argumentative nature of their relationship.

- When going to the apartment with the Humes prior to the funeral, Jay knew exactly where Maggie's ring was. How could he have known that it wasn't on her finger when she died?

- Jay failed his polygraph and never took another polygraph that might have cleared him if he were innocent.

- Jay cannot provide an alibi for twelve hours during the time of the crime.

- Despite living five blocks from the Humes in the year after the death of Maggie, Jay never visited them. In fact, he made no contact with the family in the post-funeral period.

- The body of Maggie was concealed in the apartment. A random rapist/murderer would have attacked the victim and done his utmost to put distance between him and his unknown victim. Jay would have been motivated to hide the body to put time between its discovery and the commission of the crime.

- Jay had used the balcony for entrance to the apartment numerous times before.

- Bart Thiessen's comments to his sister indicated that Jay had indicated that he had planned on murdering Maggie *prior* to her death. Jay was either conveniently or inconveniently in the vicinity at the time of Thiessen's death.

- Jay, from numerous accounts, was extremely jealous and possessive of Maggie, and this may have provided his motivation for killing her that night.

- When Detective Zuiderveen talked with Jay's mother, she asked the detective if she thought Jay had killed Maggie. This question can be taken two ways. Was she asking if police considered him a suspect, or was she asking if he had committed murder?
- In interrogation with Detective Tolf, he confided that the murder was "probably an accident." He also informed officers that Maggie had been "killed by someone she knew." He also said that Maggie was "probably killed in bed." How did Jay know any of this?
- Jay told Mrs. Hume that the flight bag with albums was missing the day after the murder. While it is possible that he knew it was gone from his search of the apartment, he had missed Maggie's body in the closet but had apparently noticed the missing flight bag.
- Jay demonstrated violence on more than one occasion regarding Maggie. In one instance, he had tried for an extended period to break into her apartment, to the point that one of the occupants armed herself with a rolling pin. Another documented instance was when he had broken the gate at the Hume home prior to Maggie moving out.
- Maggie had confided to friends that she wanted to break up with Jay but feared his violent reaction. Her reason for breaking up was that Jay was too possessive and controlling.
- Jay told Susan Schuitema at the Hume house that the door to the balcony had been picked. Investigators found no sign of that. Why would Jay say that other than to throw attention away from himself?
- Jay told Phyllis Hume that Maggie's head had been turned to the side. He had no way of knowing that—he hadn't been present when the body had been located and hadn't been told this by officers who considered him their prime suspect.
- Jay's account of Maggie asking for sex the night of her death is inconsistent with her comments to friends regarding sex. Also, Jay's account was that the blinds were open at the time. The conservative Maggie would most likely never have wanted intercourse in view of the outside. Further, Jay knew that Maggie was alone that evening and did not even offer to spend the night with her.
- The placement of the popcorn bowls on the coffee table and end table in the apartment point to the two of them sitting far apart. This seems inconsistent with a couple that had just made love.
- There was no sign of forced entry at the balcony door. Jay was the only person other than Maggie that could have made sure that door was unlocked.

- Jim Downey called several times that evening and got a busy signal, indicating that the phone was off the hook, which is inconsistent with Jay's account.
- Jay's behavior in interviews was consistent with someone who was lying. Per Detective Tolf, "When I was interrogating Jay, I asked him, 'What do you think is going to happen to you today?' He said, 'You're going to lock me up.' Innocent guys don't say that during interrogations. They say things like, 'I'll stay here all day. I'm innocent—nothing is going to happen to me!' Not Jay. That says a lot right there."
- Maggie's killer had strong hands, and Jay was a college athlete in volleyball. Per Detective Tolf, "He is imposing. An athletic guy, or he was. Six foot, muscular. He played some sport—volleyball…He was real wiry but strong. He was a type one personality. He's always the boss. He knows everything. Dominant."
- Maggie had been planting rumors that she was seeing Tom Carpenter, which may have provided the jealous Jay with a reason to kill her.
- Physical evidence (fingerprints) puts Jay in the apartment.

Factors Pointing Away from Carter as the Murderer

- The polygraph of Jay Carter may have been influenced by his interrogation hours earlier.
- The lack of an alibi is not by itself incriminating.
- There is no physical evidence to tie Jay directly to the crime. Testing the sperm recovered from Maggie would be of little use since Jay admitted that he had had intercourse with her the night of the crime.

Two different men…both tied to the same brutal murder through different journeys. One, the boyfriend, whose own statements and actions implicate him in the crime. The other, a convicted murderer, a man who confessed to the crime to satisfy his own designs. In the middle is the shattered trust between police officers and prosecutors and a family seeking only justice for a lost loved one.

Lost in the fray was Maggie Hume, the victim. Not for long, though. Murder cases don't just disappear. Cold case teams always are looking for new angles and approaches or perhaps that one missing bit of evidence or statement that drives a case home to conclusion. As the Hume case entered the twenty-first century, a new generation of officers stepped in to begin to look at it again with fresh eyes and perspectives.

EPILOGUE

When you looked at me
I should've run
But I thought it was just for fun
I see I was wrong
And I'm not so strong
I should've known all along
That time would tell.

—*"Vacation," the Go-Go's*

In 2005, Jeff Kabot, an assistant prosecutor for Calhoun County, found himself drawn into the investigation of Maggie Hume's murder. He had been working in Calhoun County since 1999 and had some exposure to the case under Prosecutor Susan Mladenoff, who had asked him to take a look at the Hume case to offer it a fresh set of eyes. Kabot didn't have ties to Battle Creek and had remained out of the fray between the BCPD and the Prosecutor's Office.

"I gathered the binders for the cases together and read them, then read them again, three…four times. It was consuming. Most people in the office really didn't know the background other than Maggie had been the daughter of the coach at St. Phil and had been strangled." He got others to sit and read the file too. The case became a focus of his time.

When John Hallacy came in as the new prosecutor, Jeff suggested the formation of a cold case team—a new set of investigators that could wade into the material. Bill Howe, a criminal investigator for the Prosecutor's

EPILOGUE

Office, outlined how the team was composed. "When we started, we had two officers from MSP, one from the Calhoun County Sheriff's Department, two detectives from the BCPD and me."

The cold case team waded into the material. It treated each suspect as the possible killer and went into what the files told it about the men it evaluated. Michael Ronning could not simply be ignored or disregarded—he lived right under her and was a killer. Mike Sherzer, now a Battle Creek City Council member and a teacher of criminal justice at Olivet College, was a member of the cold case team from the Battle Creek Police Department. He recalled how the team went in with a fresh perspective: "At no time was there any pressure at all on the cold case team by the Prosecutor's Office to consider Ronning one way or another." The team dug into Ronning's story without the political distractions that had mired the case for years. As Sherzer put it, "It's hard to deny, though, that Michael Ronning isn't an attractive candidate. Ronning was never too far away from these crimes… that makes him a compelling and attractive candidate." Sherzer, like the other members of the cold case unit (Carter Bright, Bill Howe, Barbara Walters, Randy Reinstein and Mike Jaconnette), struggled to find a way to reconcile Ronning's accounts. As Sherzer put it, "In the end, I can't make Ronning's account match up to the evidence and autopsy report."

Kabot alone spent considerable time analyzing the recordings of Ronning and the physical evidence. "Bottom line, there are thirty-seven discrepancies between what Ronning said about the Hume case and the physical evidence." This is a significant number of errors for confessions that were relatively short. Kabot's conclusions are blunt and to the point: "Michael Ronning is, at best, a con man. At worst, he wants the notoriety of being a serial killer…The only thing that Ronning got right in the Hume case was he picked the right apartment complex." The cold case team did not see him as the murderer.

That put a fresh perspective on Jay Carter as the primary suspect. Bill Howe of the Prosecutor's Office doggedly pursued Jay via the angle of the questionable auto accident that occurred only a few months after Maggie's demise. It was his digging that led to the admission of Bart Thiessen's sister that Bart had indicated that Jay had planned to murder Maggie two weeks before her death. He re-interviewed Kevin Danielson and then brought in Arthur Morrison, the man whom Kevin claimed had intimidated him into saying that Bart had been the driver of the car on the cold, windy evening. The results were a deadlock. Morrison claimed that he had never induced Kevin to say anything and that Terry had been the passenger. In the end, sadly, it came down to Kevin's word against that of the Sheerer family, who had profited from the lawsuit against Thiessen's insurance company.

Jay Carter became the focus of the cold case team. As Jeff Kabot conveyed, "Jay's own words convicted him in my mind. What he said to Mrs. Hume the next day…that 'whoever did this must have loved her…that she had been raped…and how the body was placed in the closet.' Then there's just the fact that he got involved in the search on the eighteenth. He sends John down to Margaret's room, while he goes and check's Maggie's room. He's on his knees in the closet, telling John that he knows the shoes that Maggie is likely to be wearing and her shoes were missing. There's no way he could have seen the shoes without uncovering her body." Sherzer arrived at a similar conclusion independently: "If you look at Maggie's brother's account, he says that Carter was on his hands and knees in the closet looking for shoes. There's no way he could have done that without seeing her. He insisted on going into Maggie's room. That alone points clearly to Carter. I can't explain how Jay Carter couldn't find her in that closet."

Kabot presses the matter even today, gnawing away at Jay's account of events. "Think about this. Maggie is alone for the first time. She's a Catholic girl—on her own. Sure, she's a little rebellious. According to Jay they laid down a blanket and made love on the living room floor. The shades were open. Maggie was rebellious, but not that much. Her roommate…I think it was Margaret Van Winkle…said that she put the mattress up against the wall to muffle the sounds of them making love. If she was that shy, she wouldn't have done it in full view of the window."

Jeff Kabot and the team agreed in 2007 that the only real suspect in the murder of Maggie Hume was Virgil Jay Carter. Kabot wanted to move forward with charges but was stymied by the prosecutor. According to one confidential source, John Hallacy wanted a 100 percent guarantee of a conviction. This was probably driven by the notoriety of the case and the incredible public profile after the Prosecutor's Department had been made out to be a stumbling block on *Dateline*. There was also more that complicated moving the charges forward. As Jeff Kabot put it, "We knew we'd have to prove the case, which we thought we could do. We'd also have to *disprove* the Ronning confession too."

Nancy Mullett never gave up her pursuit of Maggie's killer either, even after the turmoil of the Ronning confessions. Under the leadership of Calhoun County prosecutor Susan Mladenoff, Mullett pressed to move forward on Jay Carter. "I tried to get a Grand Jury called on Jay Carter. I couldn't get permission from the prosecutor. You have to remember, Battle

Creek is a small town, really, and there were concerns about calling a Grand Jury. I knew if we did, we'd get other people to speak out about Jay Carter. A Grand Jury would have led us to other instances of Jay's domestic violence. You don't commit domestic violence in a vacuum. You 'can' have one person that sets you off, but most of the time it's not like that—you are an abuser throughout your life." Nancy Mullett isn't bitter, but she still has a taste for justice denied.

On the twenty-fifth anniversary of Maggie's death, investigators hid a camera and audio recording device in a potted plant at Maggie's grave site. Their hope was that the murderer might visit her grave on the anniversary of her death and make an utterance or confession. All it captured was John Hume paying a private homage to his lost sister.

THE PERSON LOST IN the firestorm of accusations, insinuations and outright blunders is the victim, Maggie Hume. For her, time stopped in the early morning hours of August 18, 1982. She was denied her chance to have a life, get married and have children. She was torn away from her loving family, who were denied a chance to grow old with her.

The Hume family was almost as much a victim of this heinous crime as Maggie herself. In an interview with one of Battle Creek's newspapers, the *Enquirer*, Mike Hume expressed his desire about his daughter: "I just don't want people to forget." Nine years had passed since Maggie had been murdered, yet the wounds were still fresh for the Humes. Every Saturday, they went to Maggie's grave and left flowers. Then they would go to get dinner, where they would talk about their daughter. "I don't remember that first year much," Lorie Hume told the paper. "I'd walk by a mirror and wonder, 'Who's that sad person with tears all over her face?' I didn't go into a store for the first three or four years. I was afraid someone would talk about it." The Humes had gone so far as to hire a private investigator and a psychic. "It's the not knowing that gets us," Mike told the reporter. "People are cruel, but not intentionally. Invariably someone will come up and say, 'Hey Coach, did they catch your daughter's murderer yet?'"

Mrs. Hume conveyed, "The month of August is bad. I get jumpy or irritable. I'm always glad when fall comes."

"We'd just like it solved."

Mike Hume, Maggie's iconic father, passed away in 1997 and was buried next to his daughter. He was such a beloved figure in Battle Creek that a street was named for him, Mike Hume Way. On the twenty-fifth anniversary of Maggie's death, the local newspaper ran an interview with the Hume family.

EPILOGUE

Her brother, John, remembered, "It's been 25 long years, but sometimes it seems like it was just yesterday. A day doesn't go by that we don't think about her. It's been such a long time, but now she is with my dad and she is not alone anymore."

AS AUTHORS, WE GET the question all of the time, even from the people we interview: "Who do you think killed Maggie?" Having interviewed numerous prosecutors and officers, the authors couldn't find a single person other than Mullen and Newman who even remotely believe that Michael Ronning was connected to the death of Maggie Hume. That doesn't mean that Ronning didn't do it—simply that the case made for him doesn't sway anyone other than these two former officers.

Dennis Mullen's association with Michael Ronning was not your "typical" convicted killer/police officer relationship. Mullen gave him his home and work telephone numbers and accepted collect calls from him. They exchanged Christmas cards and correspondence. Mullen commented in an interview with one of the authors, "I was on his side." That's telling. What was needed was someone to be on Maggie's side.

By several accounts, Mullen and Newman had become so focused that Ronning had to be the killer in these three murders that they had lost their objectivity. Their motivations began as zeal to bring Maggie Hume's family justice. As one investigator shared with us, "Mullen and Newman—they believed in their investigation so much they were blinded...so convinced that anything that was against their conclusion was wrong." Even today, Newman's stance is firm. "Everyone wasted time looking into Jay Carter. There isn't a lick of evidence against Jay Carter."

Somewhere along that journey, their motivations changed. Newman confided, "We were planning on writing a book on this." In their trips to New York to meet with the *Dateline* producers and in their leaks to the press, they had painted themselves as the last two honest cops against a corrupt Prosecutor's Office hell-bent on keeping innocent men in prison. In their eyes, that is likely the reality. Rather than focus on solving the Hume murder, they wrote themselves into the saga of Maggie's murder like characters in their book that was never written. Once that happened, objectivity became simply another victim in the case.

Their steadfast focus on Michael Ronning, even in the light of court rulings that labeled him as a false confessor, made pursuit of any other suspect, including Jay Carter, more complicated. The rift they generated going to Channel 41, appearing in court against the Calhoun County

Michael Ronning as he appeared recently. His confession was never accepted as the truthful account of what happened to Maggie Hume. *Courtesy of the Arkansas Department of Corrections.*

Prosecutor's Office and involving legislators both locally and nationally in the case was bound to leave long-lasting scars. Joe Newman's argument remains: "We had an adversarial relationship with the Prosecutor's Office. If they agreed that Ronning had done the crimes, it was the same as them admitting that they had wrongly prosecuted Thomas Cress." In reality, they caused the rift with the Calhoun County Prosecutor's Office. To accept their story, you must also embrace that there was a massive conspiracy with four generations of prosecutors and assistant prosecutors against the only two individuals in law enforcement who knew the "truth."

While it has all of the elements of a good Hollywood film, reality is often much more simple. When Jeff Kabot began his own quest into the case, he found the animosity still festering there. "Things were so bad that we had to threaten to subpoena the evidence in the Hume case from the police department. We met with Mike DeBoer and told him that if they didn't turn it over, we'd subpoena it. We knew that would not play well in the press. He said, 'Don't do that,' and turned it over. That's how bad things were between us and the police department." In small cities like Battle Creek, frayed egos and battered careers were not easily forgotten.

So, as authors and researchers, who do we think did it? That doesn't matter. The facts are out there now for you, as a reader, to digest. Our opinions as authors mean little. A book like this on a case this sensitive is bound to upset a few people—that was not our intention when we began this project. Our focus has to remain simple. We remain, like you, looking for answers. Who killed Maggie Hume and why? How have they evaded capture all of this time? Where was the justice that she deserves? We, like many others, want concrete answers.

Mike Sherzer helped us in coping with this during our many interviews: "I teach criminal justice at Olivet College. One thing I tell my students is you don't get all of your questions answered in a case. There's always some uncertainty."

It is those unanswered questions that we leave to you. Someone out there knows something that has never been reported in this case. Until they've digested this book, perhaps they may not know that they possess that one little nugget of information that could change the mire into which the Hume murder has fallen. At the time, this information may have seemed inconsequential. Now, in the context of this book, it may seem important.

One of you may hold the key to solving this case and bringing justice to a young woman trapped in the autumn of 1982, frozen in time, forever young.